First published in London, 2021 by Dog Section Press,
a worker-owned cooperative

Printed by Calverts Ltd., a worker-owned cooperative

ISBN 9781916036574

Book design by Matt Bonner • revoltdesign.org
Dog Section Press logo by Marco Bevilacqua

ABOLISHING THE POLICE

Edited by
KOSHKA DUFF

Illustrated by
CAT SIMS

CONTENTS

___

GLOSSARY

A glossary of theoretical terms, as well as further resources for engaging with the collection and its ideas – including audio versions of the texts, podcast interviews with authors, discussion questions and more – will be available online. Terms in the glossary appear in bold the first time they occur in each chapter. As this is an international collection, spellings reflect the authors' different contexts and have not been standardised.

abolitionistfutures.com/abolishing-the-police-book

INTRODUCTION

Koshka Duff

———

*The police are not the only **agents** of oppression, or the only perpetrators of violence. The purpose of the police, though, is neither to fight oppression nor to reduce violence, but to uphold 'public order' – which means the order of capital and private property, of **white supremacy**, of **patriarchy**. The category of 'criminal' exists for those who disrupt that order, and that category is expanding.*

Cops Off Campus[1]

December 2013. Thousands of students march through the university campuses of central London, determined to make the area – if only for a brief, symbolic moment – a cop-free zone. They protect themselves from police truncheons with shields painted to look like the covers of books. As images of riot police raining down blows on George Orwell's *1984* begin to circulate on social media (the BBC is more interested in reporting a burning bin), #copsoffcampus is picked up by groups around the country. It will not be the last time.

I begin with Cops Off Campus because, in a sense, that is where this book began. It was there that I first met Craig Clark, who went on to found Dog Section Press – although we only really got to know each other a few months later at Highbury Magistrates' Court where, along with several of my friends, he was prosecuted for his part in the protests. The demonstration had been called in response to the university management's increasingly regular use of the police to stifle dissent on campus – and in particular, to suppress a vibrant and growing campaign by cleaners and other **outsourced** workers for sick pay, holidays and pensions. The conditions these workers (predominantly migrant women) faced within the profit-driven university included routinely unpaid wages as well as bullying and sexual harassment. In the months leading up to the Cops Off Campus mobilisation, cleaners' **picket lines** had been hassled by police. The president of the students' union had been arrested for organising a protest without consulting the police. A student (me, in fact) had been arrested and charged with criminal damage for publicising a rally in chalk on the wall of a university building. And just the night before, riot police had been called to evict an occupation in support of the cleaners' demands, with officers filmed punching students in the face.

Still fresh in our minds was the time a few years earlier when cleaners fighting for the living wage at the nearby School of Oriental and African Studies (SOAS) had been called into an apparently routine meeting with management only to be met by immigration enforcement officers hiding behind the curtains. Several trade union organisers had been deported by the end of the day. Many remembered, too, the police truncheons and **kettles**, horse charges, mass arrests and prosecutions for public order offences – some carrying lengthy prison terms – that had been used to push through the tripling of tuition fees and the scrapping of the Educational Maintenance Allowance (a small grant to enable young people from low-income backgrounds to remain in education) in the face of popular resistance in 2010.[2]

December 2010. a high metallic wire. content exceeds phrase.

What we were learning was that any attempt at emancipatory social change – or simply to resist the imposition of even more miserable and insecure conditions on the already miserable and insecure, and the plunging of more people into those conditions – was going to come up against the police. Meanwhile, the inquest into the police shooting of Mark Duggan in Tottenham, which had provoked uprisings across the country in August 2011, was coming to an end. Its official upshot: lawful killing. The court ruled that a police officer shooting an unarmed black person dead in the street does not count as breaking the law.[3] (By contrast, participants in the uprising had been fast-tracked through 24-hour courts and handed draconian sentences, often without trial or access to independent legal advice; one teenage girl, for instance, was given eight months in prison for shoplifting items including a bottle of Lucozade and some sweets.)[4] The day the verdict was announced, another

Cops Off Campus protest, larger than the first, marched to the High Court to chants of 'Police are murderers!' and 'Who killed Mark Duggan? You killed Mark Duggan!'

early 2012. the latest news is / political flashes superimposed on our rooftops

As the authors of a more recent Cops Off Campus project write,

> the best arguments against policing come from paying careful, sustained, and rigorous attention to several points: what police actually do, the conditions that make them possible, who benefits most directly from policing, and whose lives are negatively impacted by it.[5]

So, while this collection may begin with a bunch of students in central London, that is not where it stays. Looking at *what the police actually do* and *whose lives are negatively impacted* means looking beyond the more spectacular, visible moments of policing we find at demonstrations. It means paying attention to the 'experiences of everyday policing' that, as Vanessa Thompson notes in her contribution to this volume, 'often go unnoticed and unseen by large parts of society'.

One task of this book is to make more people *see* – see the oppressive violence that goes into upholding what passes for order (despite the disorder and trauma it spells for many); and see how things might be otherwise, imagine a world without that violence. Here I want to reflect a bit on why this is so hard to do. There is, in general, a vast epistemic gulf between those who experience themselves as *protected* by the police and those who are *policed* by them. The term 'epistemic' means: to do with knowledge and the reasons people have for holding beliefs. This gulf in knowledge, in how people view the police, exists because the realities of policing-in-practice tend to be hidden from those who are not directly subject to them.

Sometimes they are hidden quite literally. A great deal of the violence of the penal system takes place 'under the seal of secrecy', as the French philosopher and social theorist Michel Foucault put it in *Discipline and Punish: The Birth of the Prison*. It goes on in the 'custody suites' of police stations, behind the barbed wire walls of detention centres miles from the nearest town, in the backs of prisoner transport vans with blacked-out windows. When news of a policing operation does appear in the mainstream media, usually only the police rendition of events is permitted. The extent to which this official story is routinely and flagrantly fabricated can be hard to believe. If you and your loved ones have never had to stand in a dock and watch officer after officer line up to swear you attacked them when you *know* the opposite is true, then it can, quite understandably, be difficult to comprehend that this happens every day. (Although the findings of the recent Hillsborough inquiry,[6] and the fact that the London Metropolitan Police were able to send lorryloads of documents detailing corruption in their force to the shredders[7] with barely an eyebrow raised, do give some clue as to their mode of operation.)

Every Thursday mayhem in weather systems. / Imaginary battles in science and strike actions. The bastards had won

To learn the truth about policing, people would have to listen to the testimonies of those who have experienced it. A problem is that one of the functions of criminalisation is to exclude from public **discourse** the voices that might communicate this knowledge. The criminalised are physically excluded when they are disappeared into prisons and detention centres, or when they are shut out of education, employment or housing for having a criminal record. Labelling a person or a community 'criminal' – a derogatory term that wrongly but conveniently elides being *against the law* with being *bad, harmful, dangerous* – is also a way of discrediting them. I say 'wrongly' because, in the current unjust state of things, many things are criminalised that are not harmful (such as protesting for sick pay, holidays and pensions) and many things that are harmful are not criminalised (such as exploiting people on zero-hour contracts). I say 'conveniently' because the widespread assumption that 'criminal' equals *wrong* and *mindless* and *not to be listened to* serves very well to maintain this unjust state of things (and the wealth and power of the wealthy and powerful) by stigmatising anyone who falls foul of it.[8]

I dunno, I'd like to write a poetry that could [...] make visible whatever is forced into invisibility by police realism

The observation that dominant beliefs and ways of thinking are often rather convenient for those in power is captured in the Marxist concept of **ideology**, which various authors in this book make use of. While the word 'ideology' is often used in ordinary language simply to refer to any set of political beliefs, or sometimes as an insult for views the speaker finds dogmatic or unappealing, the word also has a more technical meaning that is relevant here. In several critical traditions, including feminism and critical race theory, the term 'ideology' refers to (a) false, misleading and distorted beliefs and ways of thinking that (b) function to prop up an oppressive **status quo** by (c) making it appear natural, just, **legitimate**, or unchangeable.[9]

To work out whether a belief is ideological in this sense we have to ask: what *effects* does it have for people to believe it? Who *benefits* from people believing it? To give an example, in late medieval Europe the belief that the monarch was appointed by God served to uphold the **hierarchical** social order of the time. It encouraged people to accept the decrees of those at the top as divinely ordained and therefore legitimate. We can observe that ideological views are often widespread or mainstream in any given time or place. This is in part because those with more wealth and power are able to control what is printed or broadcast in the media, what is put onto school curricula, what research gets funding, who gets selected for high-profile roles, and so on.

the gravitational pull that holds the entire system of hierarchical harmony together is an untruth, but an untruth with the power to kill

As well as often being literally hidden, then, the violence of policing can be hidden by ideology. Indeed, even those directly implicated in carrying it out (namely, the police themselves) may fail to *see* the reality of what they are doing insofar as they have absorbed an ideological notion of 'the criminal' that discredits and dehumanises the people they target.[10] It can also be hidden through its very effectiveness as a method of social control. This is because whenever a threat alone is enough to generate compliance, the violence backing up the threat is made less visible. If the violence backing up an order is so normalised, so taken for granted that it does not even need to be explicitly spelled out, the very nature of the order *as a threat* may disappear from view. This generates the (misleading, ideological) appearance of consent.

In my experience, something that police officers like to say to you is: do this willingly *or else*. Walk into the prisoner transport vehicle *or we'll drag you*. Take off your clothes *or we'll tie you up and cut them off with scissors*. Give us your fingerprints *or we'll take them by force and maybe break your fingers in the process*. It's your choice, they say. If this ends up being violent, you'll only have yourself to blame. A point made vividly by the #MeToo movement, however, is that whether something is consensual or coerced depends on what would happen if you decided you didn't want to go along with it. What consequences would you suffer if you declined this 'invitation'? Consent is only meaningful if there is the genuine option to *dis*sent.

the morality of our achievements, singing on the scaffold / & the riot squad have denied everything

The flip side of this is that refusing to comply with an order (in both senses of 'order') – making a fuss, disrupting business-as-usual – can sometimes make manifest the violence that was implicit in it all along. This is a reason why *knowledge of* a system and *resistance to* that system so often go hand in hand, as the anti-police protests that kicked off globally in 2020 demonstrate. By refusing to go quietly, behave nicely and take it lying down, these uprisings have burst the previously unseen violence of policing into mainstream consciousness. The realities of **structural racism** enacted by the police and penal system have been made visible precisely through the process of fighting back against them; the need for change has been illuminated in the glow of burning police precincts. As Black Lives Matter co-founder Patrisse Cullors puts it,

> This is the first time we are seeing […] a conversation about defunding, and some people having a conversation about abolishing the police and prison state. This must be what it felt like when people were talking about abolishing slavery.[11]

the point is a total reworking of all definitions / that means history, senses, cellular matter

Making a book both rigorous and accessible is not easy and I want to say a bit more here about how we have thought about and approached this challenge. This collection is written by people who have experienced and borne witness to state violence, have been part of struggles against it, and write out of commitment to those struggles. This commitment brings with it a political responsibility to write in a way that is not academic in an exclusionary sense. Many people with crucial insights into the realities of the current system and how to resist it, knowledge gained at the sharp edge of policing, do not have the privilege of academic training. An **analysis** of the injustices of policing that was inaccessible to them would be self-defeating.

On the other hand, denying ourselves the use of any vocabulary that might be unfamiliar to readers would mean discarding many powerful tools for understanding and fighting oppression. Concepts like ideology, like **racial capitalism**, **disciplinary power** and **intersectionality** – these are weapons honed over decades and even centuries of rebellious theory-making, devised and tested and contested in the context of real political struggles. To throw them away limits the thoughts we can express. It limits our ability to say true things about the police (and what is wrong with them and what we can and should do about it). It is also patronising as well as simply inaccurate to assume an inability or unwillingness to engage in complex thinking on the part of those outside of academic institutions.

science, patience, torture: the vows of the sun and the sea

We have wanted to make this book an introduction in the literal sense of *leading in* (the word comes from Latin *introducere,* where *intro-* means 'to the inside' and *ducere* means 'to lead'). We have therefore used theoretical terms where they are necessary to express ideas that we think are important, while making sure that potentially unfamiliar words are clearly explained. Explanations are included in the text where possible and also in the online glossary that accompanies the book. Terms in the glossary appear in bold the first time they occur in each piece. In these ways, we invite readers to learn to speak new critical languages. Insofar as these are still languages of the powerful, used to exclude and marginalise, we want to subvert them to speak (and enable others to speak) to the relatively privileged in ways they cannot so easily dismiss. We believe this is one way to bridge the epistemic gulf mentioned earlier, between the protected and the policed – a strategy not superior to but in solidarity with other ways of bridging this gulf also mentioned earlier, such as setting fire to police stations.

bacterial princes / shifted / rivets of history

At the same time as being widely readable, this collection breaks new theoretical ground. It does so particularly through the simultaneously broad-scoped and fine-grained account of policing it develops. This is an analysis that comprehends, as Connor Woodman and I wrote in a recent article, that:

> Policing [...] includes the whole criminal punishment system of courts, prisons, juvenile detention facilities, electronic tagging. It includes the mechanisms of border enforcement such as detention centres, walls

and barbed wire fences, chartered deportation flights. It spreads into the most intimate aspects of life in the form of mass and targeted surveillance, and it spreads beyond state boundaries in the form of colonial and **neo-colonial** 'counter-insurgency' operations, the **pacification** of unruly populations, and the '**extraordinary rendition**' of terror suspects.[12]

The volume begins with three chapters that lay out clearly why such an expansive understanding of policing is essential. Chris Rossdale explains how police power relates to **militarism** and the arms trade. Arianne Shahvisi investigates 'everyday bordering' as a form of policing into which we are all co-opted. Tom Kemp and Phe Amis write about the need to join up campaigns against border violence with those opposing prisons and practices of criminalisation more broadly.

Then come two chapters presenting what we might think of as the core, or the bread and butter, of any critical analysis of policing. We learn *what the police are there for* in Connor Woodman's account of the political function of the police to 'defend and constitute hierarchical social relations, cleavages of race, class and gender which pulsate through the social body'. We learn *where the police came from* in Tanzil Chowdhury's history of the origins of contemporary policing in colonial methods of repression and social control.

1829. Robert Peel invented 1000 pigs to circle the city as walls or gates as cordons.

To constitute something means to *make it up* in both the sense of (a) being an essential part or component of it, a building-block without which it could not exist, and (b) producing or creating it, making it exist in the first place. To say that the police help to *constitute* social categories and identities, such as being black or being a British citizen, is to say that these categories have been produced historically through the violence of policing and would not continue to exist (at least not with anything like their current shape and meaning) were it not for this ongoing violence. In the words of sociologist Stuart Schrader, 'Race is not racism's predetermined object; it is what racism produces.'[13]

This is a thought that recurs throughout this collection, but it can be a difficult one to get our heads around. Categories of race, gender, and so on have such a profound impact on experiences and life prospects in our current social order that it is easy to forget that dividing human beings up in these ways is not natural and automatic. Many use the word '**racialised**' to bring out the ways that racial identities are actively created, as Nikhil Pal Singh writes, through 'the formation and institutionalization of structures and situations of protection and vulnerability for which post hoc [i.e. after the fact] description of dishonored groups serves as a form of rationalization or justification'.[14] The authors in this volume provide numerous examples of such race-making processes. While their consequences in today's world are very real and cannot simply be imagined away, these ways of carving up humanity are not inevitable. Terms like '**naturalised**' (to make something appear natural) and 'normalised' (to make something into the norm, count as normal) make a similar point: things were not always this way and if we don't like them then – collectively – we have the power to change them.

Our understanding of how racialised categories are constructed through policing and the public discourses around it in Britain and the US today is deepened in the pieces that follow. Becka Hudson illuminates the police's constant susceptibility to far-right agitation and Eddie Bruce-Jones draws on his experiences as an educator in New York's Rikers Island prison to reflect on the difficulties of using the legal system to challenge police racism. Both bring out the close and complex relationship that has always existed between the violence perpetrated by state officials (police officers, border guards, prison wardens, and so on) and the unofficial violence meted out by far-right and white supremacist organisations and their sympathisers.

election day. terminal. a cluster of predecessors in the language / i.e. cells of racist light, in verbs, tumbling

Once we recognise just how much of taken-for-granted social reality is *made* through policing, it becomes clear that the call to abolish the police must be a genuinely revolutionary one. To what extent the orderly chaos constructed by policing could be unmade and how we might go about remaking a different world are questions taken up in the remaining chapters. Guy Aitchison and Daniel Loick examine how policing relates to law and democracy, in principle and in practice (the two often diverging dramatically). These authors diverge too, on the question of whether a genuinely democratic form of law could exist without the need for any violence to enforce it – which might prompt us to ask how far our current concepts, such as 'law', can be stretched to describe worlds so radically different from our own as to allow for truly equal participation in political decision-making.

but anyway, inside this language / there is no word for sky

Sarah Lamble and Melanie Brazzell go on then to challenge an assumption at the heart of the criminal law: that obedience to rules is the best way to understand what it means for human beings to treat each other well. They engage with the many concrete alternatives to policing – including transformative justice and community truth and reconciliation projects – that are already being practised and could be made part of our day-to-day lives in the here and now. By unpicking the '**punitive** habits and logics' that exist in our normal ways of doing things, especially the impulse always to respond to harm through the infliction of further harm, they help us to avoid the trap of policing our own movements.[15]

the present apocalypse is / a structural problem

Finally, Vanessa Thompson draws multiple strands of the book together to illuminate our current moment of crisis.

Recognising the pandemic as simultaneously exceptional and a deadly continuation of business-as-usual, and beginning from the experiences of those for whom 'I can't breathe' is not a metaphor but the result of a literal knee on the neck, she reflects on 'policing as the historical and constant condition of un-breathing' that 'renders impossible *life* for vulnerable groups all over the world'.

This is a thought I'd like to run with in a different direction. During the riotous period of factory strikes and student rebellions around May 1968, graffiti appeared across Paris:

> MEANWHILE EVERYONE WANTS TO BREATHE AND NOBODY CAN AND MANY SAY,
>
> "WE WILL BREATHE LATER."
>
> AND MOST OF THEM DON'T DIE BECAUSE THEY ARE ALREADY DEAD.[16]

The order the police enforce is brutal and **precarious** for many. It is a *racist* order, in precisely the sense defined by Ruth Wilson Gilmore: the 'state-sanctioned or extralegal production and exploitation of group-differentiated vulnerability to premature death'.[17] But for the relatively privileged who have their property and interests (in the narrow sense) protected by the police, the cop-constructed landscape of life's possibilities – 'police reality', as it is sometimes called[18] – is still dreary and uninspiring. You can dream of paying off your mortgage. You can buy John Lewis gifts for the in-laws. You can pride yourself on getting promoted in some bullshit corporate PR job you secretly know contributes nothing to the world.[19] You can twitch your net curtains and get off on the thought of those nasty teenagers getting the ASBOs they deserve.[20] The police will protect the banality of your pleasures. You may not even notice your own suffocation (this being another meaning of 'policing by consent').

babies, flags, cupcakes, brooms, victims, mummifications, the UKBA on every street corner, their guns, their illegal warrants, their racial profiles and problem families, and their scabs

Compare this with Saidiya Hartman's description of an uprising in the Bedford Reformatory, New York — December 1919. Many participants in this 'noise strike' (as the *New York Times* dubbed it) were 'wayward minors', imprisoned for their own improvement and the protection of decent society for such crimes as 'having children out of wedlock or staying out overnight or having serial lovers or intimate relations across the color line'.[21] During the riot, Hartman writes,

> Young women hung out of the windows, crowded at the doors, and huddled on shared beds sounded a complete revolution, a break with the given, an undoing and remaking of values, which called property and law and social order into crisis. [...] All of them might well have shouted, *No slave time now. Abolition now.* In *the surreal, utopian nonsense of it all*, and at the heart of riot, was the anarchy of colored girls: treason *en masse*, tumult, gathering together, the mutual collaboration required to confront the prison authorities and the

police, the willingness to lose oneself and become something greater – a chorus, swarm, ensemble, mutual aid society. In lieu of an explanation or appeal, they shouted and screamed. How else were they to express the longing to be free? How else were they to make plain their refusal to be governed?[22]

The value of resistance lies not just in what it can achieve down the line but what it manifests and is in itself – the living and breathing and singing it makes possible in the moment of its happening.[23]

don't say "tall skinny latte", say fuck the police

A few months before Cops Off Campus, I was arrested near where I lived in Hackney, London, for offering a *know your rights* legal advice card to a fifteen-year-old who was being subjected to a racist stop and search. At Stoke Newington police station I was forcibly strip searched when I refused to give the police my details.[24] While working on this introduction, I received news from my lawyer of a development in the case I have ongoing against the Met Police arising from this incident. CCTV from Stoke Newington, which the police had refused to disclose for the last seven years, had finally come to light. It captured a conversation that took place via police radio between the custody sergeant who ordered my strip search and the officers carrying it out. In a somewhat farcical misconduct hearing that took place last year, this sergeant had claimed that the strip search was motivated by concern for my safety as I 'might have had mental health problems'.[25] The contemporaneous record strikes a rather different note. 'Bend her arm then, tell her [one of the officers searching me] to put her back into it', he is heard to say. 'Do I have to come down there and do it? [...] If she's resisting, resistance is futile. By any means necessary, treat her like a terrorist, I don't care...'

The conviction that the police are fundamentally a force for good, 'your friend and helper' as the German police tagline has it, is one form that ideology takes. Another, however, is the belief that the police may be oppressive and unjust but there is nothing we can do about it. On this view, policing is all-powerful and inescapable. If we disobey, we will be destroyed. *Resistance is futile.* While these attitudes are, in a sense, polar opposites, the end result of holding them may be *conveniently* similar. Whether you lie back and think of England out of complacency or out of despair, both serve to reproduce the system.[26]

The time has come now to forget all those books written by foolish bastards who tell you to stay in your home and not listen to your hunger.

Against such a narrative, the pieces in this volume show that resistance to policing is as old as policing itself. And just as policing is not always spectacular or easily visible, so too is resistance. From community police monitoring projects to groups writing letters to prisoners, renters unionising against evictions to friends sharing tips for evading corporate revenue protection officers, *seeing* the resistance that takes place often unreported and without fanfare is crucial to countering the ideological illusion that police reality is uncontested and unchangeable. That is why 'we must recognise and support everyday resistance to police governance – on street corners, in schools, in cells – as part of our collective political action', as Tom Kemp and I wrote not so long ago.[27]

There are echoes here of the Cops Off Campus text with which I began: 'the category of "criminal" exists for those who disrupt that order, and that category is expanding'. Expanding the category of the criminal is of course something the state can do, and will always do in times of crisis – by criminalising more activities, dragging more people through the courts, putting more communities under surveillance. But it is also something that *we* can do – by refusing to be divided from each other, physically and ideologically, in the ways the law wants. That is the point of another slogan of '68: WE ARE ALL "UNDESIRABLES".

we visit you secretly / we circles of cancelled stars, we flying rags of brutal factory girls

As well as solidarity with those being criminalised right now, opposition to state violence has always been animated by practices of remembrance, or solidarity with the past.[28] Each year the United Friends and Families Campaign marches in memory of loved ones killed by the police, determined to carry on the fight for truth and accountability. Outside the walls of detention centres, protesters recite the names of those who have died inside. In this tradition, Craig and I want to dedicate this book to lost friends, of whom there are too many – and especially to Sean Bonney (1969-2019), poet against police reality, whose words burst through the cracks of this text and the cracks in the world it can no longer bear.

back now to our studies. negation of the negation. we'll raise the dead.[29]

———————

Koshka Duff is a lecturer in philosophy at the University of Nottingham with interests including social and political philosophy, German philosophy, and philosophy of music. She participates in strikes, protests and other forms of struggle around education, housing, sexual and reproductive justice, and policing, and was a co-organiser of Cops Off Campus. She is also a pianist and translator of poetry.

MARTIAL POLITICS, POLICE POWER
ABOLITION, WAR AND THE ARMS TRADE

Chris Rossdale

Every other September, the London Borough of Newham plays host to one of the world's largest arms fairs. Defence and Security Equipment International (DSEI) brings 'the entire defence manufacturing supply chain together with the world's key military specifiers, influencers, buyers, and end-users'.[30] On display is everything from tanks to tear gas, border security systems to drones, flak jackets to rocket launchers. It is a major event in the business of the international arms industry, drawing over 1,700 exhibitors and representatives from over 100 countries. Consequently, it attracts major protests aimed at stopping the event from taking place.[31]

DSEI is a site where multiple registers of policing overlap. The event takes place inside ExCeL, half exhibition centre, half fortress, which was constructed precisely in order to host highly secure events such as these. This citadel towers over the neighbouring streets. Newham is one of London's poorest boroughs, where residents are subjected to highly **racialised** policing and the constant threat of immigration raids. Protests against DSEI also face aggressive responses from police, who carry out mass arrests and target people of colour in particular. Alongside this policing of local populations and anti-DSEI protestors, the arms fair itself is an important site of policing. It is a nodal point in the global circulations of technology and expertise, and accompanying **ideologies** of order and security, that are integral to police power.

When we talk about police abolition, our focus often settles on the first two of those registers – the policing of poor communities and protests. Here we find *the* police, the institutions and their functionaries that uphold the social order, protect private property, repress dissent, and preserve the social **hierarchies** and vulnerabilities that capitalism produces and on which capitalism relies. As the other chapters in this book powerfully show, those institutions must be abolished. However, in this chapter I want to think through the third register of policing, that manifested in the arms fair itself. This is both because it is the condition of possibility of the first two, but also because it helps us to see beyond the police as a discrete institution in order to reflect on the generalisation and globalisation of policing as a practice. Doing so positions a wide range of practices including war and military action as operations of 'police power', broadening the scope and imperatives of abolition.

It has become a popular refrain to **critique** the **'militarisation'** of the police, noting the widespread and often spectacular incorporation of military equipment, tactics and aesthetics into domestic police forces.[32] These critiques usefully outline the processes through which police forces are continually reorganised to administer violence. However, they are also problematic inasmuch as they imply the existence of a virtuous non- or pre-militarised police.[33] One response, as we see in Tanzil Chowdhury's contribution to this volume, is to show that police forces have *always* been military actors, have always engaged in war-like relations with marginalised **subjects**. Such readings frequently use the metaphor of a boomerang, where technologies and techniques trialled within colonies including Ireland, South Africa and the Philippines returned to be used against populations in the metropoles of the **Global North**, including the US and UK.[34] In this **analysis**, policing in the West is a site of colonial power coming home, the extension of colonial wars to domestic populations. These responses are valuable, but the direction of analysis can also be reversed. Alongside recognising the martial and colonial nature of police forces we might also pay careful attention to the organisation of war and military force through police power. For some insights on this we can turn to the thought of Huey P. Newton, founder and leader of the Black Panther Party (BPP).

The BPP emerged in response to the daily violence meted out to Black people by US police forces. Newton and his comrades recognised that this violence was integral to the maintenance of a capitalist system that was (and is) predicated on keeping the majority of Black Americans insecure and vulnerable to exploitation. As such, they understood the revolutionary implications of police abolition.[35] One of the features that distinguished the Panthers' analysis was that they conceptualised their encounters with the police in the ghetto in both international and colonial terms.[36] Black Americans were a *colonised* people, subjected to occupation by a foreign and hostile power, of which the police were 'the foot-soldiers in the trenches of the ghetto'.[37] They saw close connections between their own experience and those of others subjected to US imperial power; politically and ethically there was no **substantive** distinction between the actions of the police and national guard towards Black people in US cities and those of the US army in Vietnam. As Newton recalled, '[w]e…viewed the local police, the National Guard, and the regular military as one huge armed group that opposed the will of the people'.[38]

This understanding fuelled a firmly internationalist strategy, even while the Panthers expended most of their energies carrying out social programs in Black communities within the US. As the Panthers endured relentless state violence against their organisation, Newton began to theorise emerging shifts in global power relations. He argued that the massive military power of the US, alongside the accelerating **globalisation** of capitalist production, meant that the world was no longer meaningfully divided into separate nations.

The autonomy and decision-making capacities of individual states had become subsumed by the coercive power of global markets and US **hegemony**.[39] This motivated a shift in Panther strategies. National liberation was no longer a meaningful goal in a world dominated by this new form of empire; instead, a global network of insurgent communities was the goal.

There are a number of implications of this new framework, which, as John Narayan shows, anticipated emerging accounts of **neoliberal** globalisation.[40] I'm most interested in how Newton's new theory – which he terms **intercommunalism** – shifts our understanding of policing. The global spread of capitalism and waning power of individual states, alongside developments in technologies of production, communication and **pacification**, entailed a new global dimension of policing: '[t]he "police" are everywhere and they all wear the same uniform and use the same tools, and have the same purpose: the protection of the ruling circle here in North America'.[41] Within Newton's framing, the police are always local, carrying out brutal violence in ghettos and jungles and townships and favelas, but also global, enlisted in upholding capitalist social relations and constituted through transnational or intercommunal circulations of training, equipment, expertise, ideology.

So, for Newton, the police doesn't only mean *the* police. There is no real difference between police officers in Oakland, national guardsmen in Detroit, GIs in Vietnam, prison officers in Soledad.[42] Importantly, he recognises the evolution of warfare into a form of police activity: '[t]he ruling circle no longer even acknowledges wars; they call them "police actions". They call the riots of the Vietnamese people "domestic disturbance."'[43] As others have since pointed out, much that passes under the banner of war and military action might be more appropriately described as a form of policing, inasmuch as it is directed towards the management and administration of global capitalism, and the targeted response to elements that threaten to unsettle that system.[44] By this measure military interventions, peacebuilding missions, overseas bases, counter-insurgency operations, all operate as a form of global policing, guided by the promise to preserve or impose order, to retain or guarantee security. This is a framing that has become popular amongst both critical theorists and military actors, albeit for very different reasons, with the former trying to make sense of the shifting nature of global power, the latter keen to mobilise a **discourse** that may be more palatable than outright war.[45] What Newton does is recognise the mutual inseparability of policing and war. Neither has *become* the other. Instead, the two are always mutually entangled; police forces operate in war-like relations with marginalised communities, while warfare is shaped and guided by police power.

It is Mark Neocleous who encourages us to think in terms of 'police power', by which he means a 'whole range of technologies [that] form the social order', pacifying unruly, disobedient and criminalised subjects.[46] Police power is the administration of **structural violence** – the institutions and practices through which those on the margins of the economic and political system are disciplined, pacified, excluded, or exterminated. It operates on the terrain of security and order, endlessly promising their preservation or restoration, obscuring not only the ways that order and security for some is chaos and insecurity for others, but also how hegemonic standards of order and security are *reliant on* the insecurity and chaos of marginalised subjects. **Racial capitalism** is fundamentally dependent on those at its margins, those 'edge-populations'[47] who are vulnerable to exploitation and against whom more obedient or ambivalent subjects might be turned. It also depends on the exercise of police power to maintain the marginal status of these edge populations. Many different kinds of institution are implicated in police power, including militaries, border agencies, and private security firms, alongside the debt industry, mental health and social work organisations, schools, and of course police forces.[48] As others in this volume so powerfully argue, to adequately understand, critique and overthrow policing, we have to think beyond 'the police'. Police power is a useful framing in this context.

Let's return to DSEI, which exemplifies the interwovenness of military power and police power. DSEI is a carnival of global policing, helping to connect thousands of companies with state buyers from around the world (while cementing Britain's role as a key player within these industries). Cutting edge products across air, land, sea and space, are marketed to militaries, police forces, security sectors, cyber defence, and border and counter-terror agencies. Campaigners are keen to point out the obscene fact that states in conflict with one another can be found shopping in the same arms fair, but perhaps even more troubling is the fact that the buyers here are highly unlikely to use these products against one another at all; much of this equipment is designed for use against states' own populations. These are 'solutions' for dealing with uprisings, riots, liberation movements, migration flows, insurgencies. Alternatively, they are destined to be used in calamitous military interventions, or the enduring disasters of the wars on terror and drugs.[49] These prospective sales at DSEI are supplemented by training seminars, keynote talks, and fancy dinners. In this space, we see the circulation of technology, expertise and ideology, amongst a group committed to the administration of global order.

The point isn't that everyone at the arms fair is committed to a single and well-defined international project, nor that the common enemies or target populations of this 'community' are automatically virtuous. Rather, it is that through this carnival flow the equipment and expertise that will enable and shape police, border, counter-terror, military, and security forces around the world, and that these various forces tend towards the preservation of established power relations. DSEI is a nodal point of global policing, and the technologies and techniques that move through these spaces will travel around the world, some of them returning to the streets of Newham.

If we recognise this broader account of policing, then the necessity, scope and promise of police abolition expands. Abolition is not just a call for the end of **formal** police forces, but an insurrection against policing as a strategy of administering structural violence. It is a call for the abolition of an economic system, a system of racial violence, a system of endless imperial war, through which capitalist markets are protected and exploited and expendable populations held in abjection. It requires the dismantling of military institutions and the arms trade. These are clearly not small tasks – they may even seem impossible. Nevertheless, the abolitionist project is one that insists on the possibility of a radically different future. It challenges us to maintain expansive horizons even as we confront the challenges of the everyday. It demands and celebrates a ceaseless rebellion against police power, in all its forms.

Chris Rossdale lectures in politics and international relations at the University of Bristol. His research explores how radical social movements operate as incubators of critical knowledge and theory, with a particular focus on those contesting militarism and state violence. He is also involved with Campaign Against the Arms Trade and other anti-militarist projects.

WE ARE ALL POLICE NOW
RESISTING EVERYDAY BORDERING AND THE HOSTILE ENVIRONMENT

Arianne Shahvisi

———

For a month in the late summer of 2013, large, unsightly vans were driven around six London boroughs chosen for their significant immigrant populations. In block text, they paraded the message 'In the UK illegally? Go home or face arrest', which was also displayed in shop windows, health facilities, and places of worship.[50] The name of the pilot was 'Operation Vaken', whose possible Nazi undertones have been noted.[51] The scheme was a flop: there was widespread criticism, almost nobody 'volunteered' to go home, and the costs were ultimately deemed to outweigh the benefits.[52]

Despite their uselessness, the 'Go home' vans, as they came to be known, were a sign of the times. Not only had hostility towards migrants reached an alarming new fever pitch that would pave the way to the Brexit referendum three years later, but the government's tactics had become indistinguishable from those of the tabloid newspapers they had always fed. Operation Vaken was like a giant mobile *Daily Mail* headline

– brash, bullying, and brainless. Further, the vans were an inescapable reminder that the border could be brought to the streets we live on. This was not news to everyone, since raids on homes and businesses in search of irregular migrants had by this point become routine. In the years leading up to Operation Vaken, Immigration Compliance and Enforcement (ICE) teams – many of them former soldiers and police officers – carried out around 6,000 raids a year, mostly on Indian restaurants and takeaways.[53] Officers compete with each other to make the highest number of arrests, and are rewarded with cake and boxes of chocolates as their arrestees are taken to detention centres to await deportation.[54] Importantly, most of their initial leads come from members of the public, who volunteer around 50,000 tip-offs a year.[55]

Operation Vaken illustrates several patterns that are becoming increasingly noticeable in relation to bordering:

- Borders are no longer just physical barriers at the boundaries of our societies but now pervade the structures of our social world;

- Workplaces, as well as other spaces of everyday living, are now sites of bordering;

- Everyday people are now a critical part of border enforcement;

- Bordering practices are generally not undertaken for economic reasons but rather serve to communicate a particular attitude towards migrants and produce and reinforce an atmosphere of hostility.

This new form of bordering is known as 'everyday bordering'.[56] In the rest of this chapter, I briefly describe everyday bordering in the UK, illustrate its effects within the National Health Service, and emphasise the importance of resisting the ways in which it turns civilians into border police, making many of us complicit in harms against people who have a moral claim upon the benefits of membership of **Global North** states.

EVERYDAY BORDERING IN THE HOSTILE ENVIRONMENT

The year before Operation Vaken, Theresa May discussed plans to progressively reduce the public services accessible to migrants, stating that 'the aim is to create here in Britain a really hostile environment for illegal migration'.[57] The rise of everyday bordering is the staging of this ambition, and it has succeeded in producing conditions under which the lives of many migrants are severely constrained and the division between those who belong and those who do not is deeper than ever.

Historically, most interactions with borders in the UK took place in airports and seaports. Over the last fifty years, these borders have started to pervade the interior of the state. From the 1970s onwards, new legislation was introduced in successive government acts that brought a gradually wider range of services, institutions, and workers into the fold of border policing. The 2014 and 2016 Immigration Acts are the most recent of these and have made workplaces, marriages, housing, hospitals, vehicles, banks, schools, and universities sites of bordering.[58] The idea has been to corner irregular migrants, to ensure that their interactions with essential services are difficult and hostile, and to produce additional opportunities for surveillance, detection, and arrest. Irregular migrants are now forbidden from working, driving, and renting, and are required to pay prohibitive fees for hospital care.

Everyday bordering does not replace the traditional physical, situated borders, but extends them. This requires new forms of surveillance and bureaucracy, and the additional labour is outsourced to those working within the services that the recent Immigration Acts target, who face fines or prosecution for failure to fulfil their new border duties. Devolving border policing in this way saves money, allows a greater geographical coverage, and entrenches bordering as part of our social world by making it an ordinary activity of a wide range of workers. As a result, a constellation of different **agents** are now complicit in the harms of the border regime, most of whom receive no additional training or pay for this onerous and distressing new duty.

Requiring that employers, bank workers, landlords, healthcare workers, and educational professionals check the immigration status of those they encounter also produces new opportunities for racism. Racial profiling is more readily excused, and people of colour as a whole face additional barriers to accessing services. Everyday bordering contributes to a sense of identity and security for those who are white and British, and may serve as tangible, visible reassurance that resources are being reserved for these citizens, thereby securing their political support. I refer to this phenomenon as '**conspicuous marginalisation**'. Not only are certain groups marginalised, but that marginalisation is continually announced (on the side of vans, for example) in order to win the favour of a particular target audience. Conspicuous marginalisation is an especially shrewd strategy, which has protected the government from criticism as it has continued to make cuts to welfare and public services under the last decade of austerity; migrants serve as a convenient scapegoat for any perceived scarcity, thereby providing a perpetual mandate for further draconian anti-immigrant measures.

For people of colour and migrants, everyday bordering makes racism a more entrenched property of their interactions with the state. Racist micro-aggressions (such as the loaded, **othering** question 'where are you (really) from?') acquire a new **legitimacy**, which in turn leads to an increase in more overt racist abuse (such as being subject to racist slurs or assault). While the legislation is officially intended to target irregular migrants, the **discourse** that does so is necessarily racist and therefore lacks specificity. That it spills over and also marginalises migrants and people of colour more generally is an important feature of conspicuous marginalisation: its objective is to target all those whose claim upon resources is widely held, for racist reasons, to be questionable. That so many British-born people of colour are told to 'go home' is testament to the fact that immigration status is not the only factor at work. Citizenship is therefore no protection against the racism caused by everyday bordering, even though it (mostly)[59] protects against the more extreme effects of border violence: arrest, detention and deportation.

Everyday bordering is chaotic and uneven. Its overarching aim seems to be to ensure that everyday interactions are infected with fear of the violence of borders. Employers, landlords, and medical professionals are often not well-informed about their precise duties and may under- or over-apply the official guidelines. This can lead to people being turned away from services they are in fact entitled to use. The fact that it functions so variably is a clue that its precise details are less important than its discursive effect. In the following case study, this point is made vivid.

CASE STUDY: BORDERING IN THE NHS

While the UK's National Health Service (NHS) was founded on the commitment to free healthcare for all delivered solely on the basis of need, the Immigration Acts of 2014 and 2016 revoke that principle. It is now a complex, multi-tier system in which all those who are not 'ordinarily resident' in the UK must pay for at least some of their care. Being 'ordinarily resident' means being able to show that you have lived in the UK for five years with documentation. All 'visitors' and irregular migrants must pay for anything other than the most basic care. This means that an irregular migrant who becomes pregnant in the UK must pay £7,000 for pregnancy care,[60] while cancer treatment can cost as much as £54,000.[61]

Irregular migrants are entitled to free primary care and may therefore see a general practitioner (GP) without charge. In reality, many choose not to, for fear of attracting attention from state authorities. Those who do seek healthcare have often waited years, by which point they may have developed serious complications. Referrals to hospital (except in the case of an immediate medical emergency) do incur charges, and if medical debts are unpaid after two months, patient information is shared with the Home Office. This places GPs in the difficult position of recommending essential care for medical reasons but knowing that patients will likely be unable to afford the financial and legal consequences, and may therefore be unwilling to assent to referral to other services. As with other workers who must now contend with everyday bordering, doctors may experience moral distress as their patients refuse essential care.[62]

Importantly, all the available data shows that charging migrants for their care does not save the NHS money.[63] Rather, the cost of administrating the new system far outweighs the savings made, which is further evidence that bordering within the NHS feeds and is fed by xenophobia, rather than being a frugal policy decision. This suspicion is more broadly borne out by the observation that the government ensures 'hard borders', and caps on immigration are ever-present in political discourse, despite knowing that migrants of all stripes are net contributors to the UK economy. From 2000 to 2011, they brought in £25 billion, while non-migrant citizens made a *negative* contribution of £617 billion over the same period.[64]

BORDER IMPERIALISM

At the heart of everyday bordering is the idea – largely unquestioned in British political discourse – of irregular migrants as criminals. On a trivial reading, irregular migrants are indeed criminals, since they have entered, or remained, in the UK in contravention of law. This criminality is more or less unavoidable for many people seeking to live in the UK since legal entry is all but impossible and around half of all asylum applications are rejected.[65] Yet public discourse around immigration encourages a much more loaded, derogatory conception of their criminality, portraying irregular migrants as automatically morally deplorable by virtue of their desire to access the benefits of UK society. Misunderstandings also proliferate, adding outright falsehoods to an already dubious discourse. Contrary to public opinion and the implications of some popular media, irregular migrants cannot claim welfare payments, under-use even those public services to which they are entitled, and are often exploited to work for less than minimum wage.

The criminality discourse in relation to migrants is complex and deserves careful **analysis**. On one side, the government and tabloid media insist upon the criminality of irregular migrants and also gesture towards the moral inferiority of migrants more generally. They are criticised both for working ('stealing jobs') or not working ('scrounging') and are often deemed to make insufficient attempts to adhere to 'British culture' – a concept so vague, and referring to ways of life that are so heterogeneous, as to be meaningless. (Grudging acceptance is sometimes extended to migrants of the 'right' kind, usually meaning those who work in the NHS.)

On the other side, those who sympathise with irregular migrants sometimes resort to defending their innocence, insisting that they are not criminals. This too has its problems. First, it's false. Most *are* criminals, in the literal sense that they have committed a criminal act by entering or remaining in the UK. Second, in resisting the label of criminality there is a tendency to over-emphasise the victimhood of irregular migrants in ways that appeal to the consciences of British people, who are often most willing to accept narratives that play on the 'backwardness' of the cultures from which migrants originate.[66] Further, irregular migrants are often presented as innocent, good, honest people, which is not only an unrealistic portrayal (negative character traits are present in every human group) but also reinforces the troubling idea that only those migrants who are deemed to be 'good' should be afforded membership and access to essential resources – a standard that is not applied to non-migrants in the UK. Third, the insistence that *they* should not be called criminals tends to more firmly emphasise that *others* should be. This entrenches the legitimacy of criminalisation more generally – calling out the misuse of a concept usually has the effect of bolstering its reasonableness in other cases. In doing so, we risk missing an important opportunity to see parallels between those criminalised by borders and those criminalised by other apparatuses of inequality.

The 'criminality' of irregular migrants is just a special case of the questionable concept of criminality more generally. In a great many cases, 'criminals' are those who are deprived not only of certain essential goods that are necessary to their wellbeing and dignity, but also of any socially or legally acceptable routes to accessing those goods. It has been known for decades that inequality leads to higher crime rates, with more unequal societies having higher levels of social unrest.[67] The privatisation of tremendous amounts of wealth reduces the opportunities others have for dignified lives, necessitating criminality. Borders are the ultimate mechanisms of inequality. They enclose and protect concentrations of wealth in Global North regions and make trespassers of those who try to access that wealth.

The criminality framing also disregards the reasons why people seek residence in the UK in the first place, presenting migrants as agents of harm rather than as victims of prior harms. Three-quarters of those arrested in immigration raids are from Bangladesh, Pakistan, and India,[68] while asylum applicants are primarily from Iran, Iraq, or Pakistan.[69] What do these states have in common? Their current political and economic situations have been strongly influenced by British colonialism and by more recent military **imperialism**. A state being a former colony is a strong predictor of it now being characterised by repressive governance, widespread poverty, and conflict.[70] The UK has made many **Global South** countries places where most people cannot meet their needs and live with dignity.

Colonialism has always had a complex relationship with borders: settler colonialism is founded on disregarding others' territorial claims and enforcing new borders of convenience. As British settler colonialism began to be dismantled in the twentieth century, the UK closed its borders to most of those who had once been its subjects.[71] This ensured that the wealth of the former empire remained concentrated in the metropole, for the benefit only of its own citizens, while its former territories lay ransacked and contending with the inevitable chaos and conflict of gerrymandered borders. Accordingly, not only do many migrants have a moral claim upon the resources they migrate in search of, but their supposed crime – of crossing borders – is necessitated by Britain having expediently disregarded borders in order to amass the wealth that now makes it such a desirable destination for migrants.

RESISTING EVERYDAY BORDERING

Everyday bordering does not go unchallenged. Various protests have accompanied attempted immigration raids,[72] and medical professionals have called for an end to bordering within the NHS.[73] Organisations such as Docs Not Cops, Anti Raids Network, Freedom from Torture, Joint Council for the Welfare of Immigrants, Undoing Borders, and Women for Refugee Women, to name just a few, work to seek justice for irregular migrants and pressure the government and media to shift the damaging anti-migrant discourse that is now orthodoxy in the UK. However, a larger, joined-up movement will be required to resist everyday bordering as it continues to creep into all of our lives.

One exemplary template for cross-sectoral resistance may be found in the 'Patients not Passports' toolkit developed as a collaboration between three health and migration charities,[74] which provides step-by-step guidance for healthcare workers to resist bordering in the NHS, while also advising communities on providing support and solidarity to those affected by the hostile environment.

Those who are able to object to their new border duties ought to do so. Happily, many of those who have been asked to take on new border policing roles are those with considerable social power (e.g. landlords, doctors, university staff) and are therefore better positioned to resist. Unhappily, it is often the case that those with social power are least likely to want to part with it by defying orders from the establishment. In academia and the NHS, many are also overworked, and **precarity** poses an additional barrier for those whose livelihoods may be at risk if they refuse to follow institutional orders. For these reasons, it is particularly important that organised resistance is given visible support by those who have the power and platforms to defend the action and generate more widespread support. Consultant doctors and high-profile academics are therefore critical to the success of any resistance movement and should acknowledge and work towards realising that duty.

All the while, we must destabilise the bordered logic that treats migrants as criminals and citizens as instruments of state power, which requires continual discussion of the realities of everyday bordering, an appreciation of the lessons of history, and a well-informed fear of the future we're heading towards.

Arianne Shahvisi is a philosopher and writer whose work focuses on gender, race, and migration. She has been involved in activism relating to austerity, migrant domestic work, and Palestine. She lectures on feminist and anticolonial ethics at the Brighton and Sussex Medical School, and is science editor for literary magazine The Offing, which amplifies the voices of marginalised writers.

WHY BORDERS *AND* PRISONS, BORDER GUARDS *AND* POLICE?

Tom Kemp & Phe Amis

———————

I n recent years, the injustices of border enforcement have become central sites of struggle for radical and left-**liberal** politics. The demand to shut down the UK's detention centres and to end 'hostile environment' policies is gaining support from a growing range of political actors. However, the predominant forms of migrant rights campaigning in the UK are still premised on the assumption that immigration detention and border enforcement are separable from prisons and police. For some, this is an **analytical** distinction. It might be held, for example, that borders target people because of *who* they are rather than *what* they have done. For others, this is a strategic distinction. It might be more imaginable to destabilise recent manifestations of borders than to eradicate other forms of policing and imprisonment.

We think that this distinction is analytically and strategically flawed. We argue that migrant rights campaigns have to incorporate radical **critiques** of policing and prisons.

Because the operation of borders, policing and prisons depend on one another. Because they maintain a global regime of **racial capitalism** that developed out of European colonialism. Because they perpetuate similar forms of violence and serve similar social functions. Because in order to realise rights and overturn historical systems of dispossession, we need to connect our struggles. This chapter is about why we cannot detach the immigration regime from prisons and policing.

THE GROWING INTER-CONNECTIONS OF BORDER ENFORCEMENT AND POLICING

Within the migrant rights movement, it is common to think of border enforcement and policing as distinct institutions. However, despite the way these institutions are separated by government departments and seem to have different purposes, the contemporary policing of borders is intimately entangled with the criminal punishment system.

In recent years, the rhetoric of 'illegality' has been used to facilitate and justify ever more **punitive** measures to police **racialised** migrant communities. A unified *Border Force* was introduced for the first time in 2007, in the aftermath of London's 7/7 bombings in 2005 and the so-called 'foreign prisoner scandal' of 2006. The scandal prompted the end of the Home Office's century-old responsibility for prisons, policing and sentencing and the formation of a newly-invented Ministry of Justice. As part of a bombastic set of anti-terrorism measures Prime Minister Gordon Brown announced in July 2007, three separate departments – UK Visas, HM Revenue and Customs, and the Border and Immigration Agency – were merged into the UK Border Agency with the remit of helping 'to track and intercept terrorists and criminals, as well as, of course, illegal immigrants'.[75] Although ordinary immigration officers are not legally 'constables', the newly-uniformed presence of the *Border Force* resembles the police enough to redouble the **affective** impact of its powers of arrest and detention over people suspected of 'immigration crimes'. Similarly, over the last four decades immigration officers have often teamed up with police forces to make the widest use of their powers through immigration raids in homes, high streets and workplaces. Such raids have been strenuously resisted by **direct action**, *know your rights* mobilisations, and organised monitoring by the racialised communities targeted. The surviving distinction on paper, and the affective distinction on the ground, between immigration officers and officers with full police powers is to the credit of this long tradition of anti-racist activism.

Meanwhile immigration detention centres have expanded tenfold since the mid-1990s and now hold up to 30,000 people per year.[76] Prisons, which hold hundreds of people post-sentence under immigration powers, function as a punitive extension of the immigration detention estate. In sum, when we look at developments over the last thirty years it seems that border enforcement has increasingly come to resemble the policing and prison system.

Likewise, in the last decade the police have visibly taken on more border control functions. As Arianne Shahvisi's chapter details, the 'hostile environment' policies implemented through the Immigration Acts of 2014 and 2016 contained numerous measures to further criminalise and obstruct the possibilities of surviving and subsisting in the UK for those without secure immigration status. These policies intensified a trend of increasing the powers of police in assisting immigration control. For example, in 2012 the Metropolitan Police piloted Operation *Nexus*, an unpublished data-sharing initiative between the Home Office and the police.[77] Under *Nexus,* police used stop and search powers to take racially profiled people into custody. In custody, newly-embedded immigration officers interviewed arrestees to find out their immigration status and compiled 'intelligence histories' for deportation cases. In a textbook application of **mission creep** strategy, *Nexus* was publicly introduced as targeting 'high harm' offenders with insecure immigration status. In reality, it allowed the police to routinely target rough sleepers, shoplifters, people encountered or reported as inebriated, psychotic or suicidal, and even people who were, in the police's words, 'victims or witnesses to violent crimes but refused to cooperate with police'.[78] Since 2006, the normalisation of the policy term 'foreign national offender' through media spectacle has in practice allowed the police to mark for deportation people whose criminality was tenuous and speculative even within the skewed frame of the UK's institutionally racist criminal punishment system.[79] Meanwhile the only mode of challenging deportation lies in the separate system of immigration tribunals that even on paper has much lower standards of evidence and fewer public-facing procedures than the criminal courts.

We highlight this not to make the point that one court system is less fair than the other, but to highlight the ways in which the distinction between 'administrative' and 'criminal' systems is part of an **ideological** strategy for differentiating and targeting specific groups for predictive policing and collective punishment while making the system labelled 'administrative' appear less draconian and therefore in need of fewer legal safeguards. This distinction originated in colonial legal systems across the British empire[80] and was imported back to the UK at the 'official' end of empire when racist immigration laws were put in place during the 1960s. The racialised distinction between administrative and criminal justice systems persists today not only in the administration of immigration law but also in the everyday administration of counter-terrorism projects that extend expressly Islamophobic policing logics to encode schools, universities, hospitals and even the (specifically Muslim) private family home as 'pre-criminal spaces' in which potential terrorists are made.[81]

In these ways, the last thirty years of changes to UK border enforcement show us an institution that has more and more looked and acted like a police force and a prison estate. But adopting a wider historical lens brings a different story into focus, one which reminds us that understanding immigration enforcement and racist policing as a single phenomenon was the common starting point for anti-racist campaigners for most of the 20th century. The shifts explored in this section are therefore part of a historical process begun in the 1970s when policing, immigration control and the state itself were reconstituted to present Britain's **imperial** and industrial collapse in terms of a 'moral decline' and a 'violent society' caused by the settlement of formerly colonised people in post-war Britain.[82]

BORDERS, PRISONS AND COLONIALITY

Migrant rights campaigners often allude to the idea that border controls have a relationship with Britain's colonial past. Immigration controls are a historical product of post-colonial European statehood, developed to mobilise 'race' to restructure entitlements to 'British' wealth accrued during five centuries of enslavement and colonisation. They are used to disavow claims of belonging by Black people and people of colour, many of whom had on paper been recognised alongside white Britons as 'Citizens of the UK and Colonies' until the 1971 Immigration Act.[83] It is used, as Nadine El-Enany has underlined, to 'teach white British people that Britain and everything within it is rightfully theirs' – the full spoils of Britain's colonial empire.[84] The borders of the UK and of the European Union are also modes of **neo-colonial** control that responsibilise states for producing migrants and export border policing duties outside of Europe, using international development funds for border policing, detention and repatriation schemes in places like the Sudan, Niger and Turkey.[85]

The relationship between today's policing and (supposedly) yesterday's colonialism is less widely appreciated by migrant rights campaigners. In this volume, Tanzil Chowdhury explains how the development of policing in Britain is intimately tied to the histories of colonial governance and resistance to colonial rule. This is evidenced in the fact that, in 1829, Home Secretary Sir Robert Peel modelled the Metropolitan Police on the Peace Preservation Force he had recently established in Ireland during his stint as Irish Secretary between 1812 and 1820. It is also seen in the consistent cross-fertilisation between Britain's domestic and colonial police forces. Police with experience of the even more violent and repressive regimes of policing in the colonies were brought to the UK to influence the culture of policing in response to the uprisings of the 1970s and 1980s. Meanwhile, the UK police sought to export its policing expertise and reform agendas to the empire and commonwealth. This pattern continues to the present day. The Royal Ulster Constabulary in the North of Ireland, which was the UK's only fully-armed territorial police force, provides the blue-print for global 'peace-keeping missions' in Iraq, Afghanistan, Bosnia and Kosovo that extend British investment in imperialism as it operates today.[86]

Perhaps more surprisingly, the connection between policing, borders and **coloniality** also includes the British empire's abolition of slavery in 1833. Both abolition and the establishment of policing in 19th century Britain were intimately entangled with the repackaging of British history and nationhood. These narratives continue to shape the racialisation of citizenship and nationality in Britain in very tangible ways. For instance, the Home Office's *Life in the United Kingdom: A Guide for New Residents* teaches applicants for British citizenship that 'in 1833 the Emancipation Act abolished slavery throughout the British Empire [and thereafter] the Royal Navy stopped slave ships from other countries, freed the slaves and punished the slave traders'.[87] In reality, legislative abolition was motivated not by humanitarian reasons but because the organised resistance of enslaved people was making British plantation economies cost-ineffective.[88] Nonetheless, Victorian imperial policy and popular culture increasingly personified Britain as 'the global policeman' both bringing law and order to an 'uncivilised' world and demonstrating Britain's moral supremacy over slave trading states.[89]

At the forefront of this imperialist rhetoric, grounded in **white supremacy**, was not only the British state but considerable parts of the organised liberal abolitionist movement. As early as 1840, prominent abolitionists had formed the *Society for the Extinction of the Slave Trade and for* *the Civilisation of Africa.* The Society mobilised its existing philanthropic networks and political campaigning tools towards preparing missionary expeditions to eradicate an African slave trade that was aggressively reframed as 'Mohammedan'. Alongside Christianity, the colonial imposition of agricultural commercial intercourse' was framed as the inculcation of 'new methods of earning wealth by honest industry' that would 'elevate the native mind' away from the immoralities of slave-trading and bring law and order to African societies.[90]

In short, although immigration enforcement has only appeared as a form of everyday policing on British soil since the constitutional end of the British empire, the United Kingdom was the administrative centre of **disciplinary violence** and racialised mobility controls upon colonised peoples elsewhere for centuries before police brutality against Black and brown people became visible in post-imperial Britain.[91]

With this longer-term view, it is no surprise that much anti-racist campaigning of the 20th century treated immigration control and racist policing as part and parcel of the same phenomenon. For Black merchant sailors, seamen of colour and their communities in British port cities in the early 20th century, everyday police harassment in the form of internal passport checks (long before passports were obligatory for crossing even external borders) was consistently flanked by police brutality and police complicity with widespread white racist street violence, most clearly during the 1919 'race riots' in Liverpool, Cardiff, Salford and Glasgow. This routine harassment was not only sanctioned but nurtured by the state's legislation of racialised immigration restrictions under the Special Restriction (Coloured Alien Seamen) Order of 1925.[92]

Likewise, the restriction of 'New Commonwealth' immigration by the Commonwealth Immigrants Act in 1962, summarised by Claudia Jones as 'an official colour bar against the coloured and the poor'[93], was protested, documented and analysed by West Indian, Pakistani and Indian mutual aid groups, political organisations and workers' associations as directly intensifying police brutality towards 'immigrant' communities.[94] For Black Power and youth movements consolidating in the 1970s and 1980s, defending Black people and people of colour against deportation, fascist violence and police harassment were inseparable parts of community self-defence.[95]

Emphasising these interconnections remained crucial to both the growing organisation of individual anti-deportation campaigns and the legal defence strategies in the political show trials of anti-racist activists such as the Mangrove 9 (in 1970) and the Bradford 12 (in 1981). As Thatcherite reforms to the welfare system took shape, the tangle of welfare office harassment and surveillance with immigration enforcement and racist policing was squarely analysed and organised against as a continuation of colonial violence and the super-exploitation of Black women's and women of colour's labour.[96] This rich and well-documented history of anti-racism in Britain[97] renders quite strange contemporary forms of liberal migrant rights and refugee solidarity campaigning, which shy away from using imperialism as a diagnostic frame and actively court respectability by reproducing the distinction between border control and policing.[98]

VIOLENCE, BORDERS AND CARCERALITY

This discussion of their shared colonial history also lays the groundwork for a further argument against treating immigration and criminal policing differently. This argument draws attention to similarities in the means of coercion that these regimes use and the function they play within the reproduction of what Cedric Robinson called 'racial capitalism' – a global system that rests on intertwined processes of racialisation and capitalist exploitation.[99]

To start with, both borders and prisons enable and legitimise brutality. In some cases, this violence is obvious and dramatic. The deaths of thousands of migrants in the Mediterranean. The execution of an enforced deportation. The policing of protest. Deaths in custody. The assertion of order within prison walls. In other cases, this brutality operates through mundane administrative control under which people wait indefinitely for the Home Office or parole boards to make unaccountable and systematically incompetent decisions that put life on hold. In the process, these institutions cultivate a mental health crisis in prisons and detention centres, which spreads to the everyday lives of friends and families.

Despite the harm inflicted by these systems, the violence exerted on illegalised and criminalised people is routinely presented as a form of care. Often this violence is perpetuated in the name of protecting 'the community' or 'society'. Border enforcement, prisons and policing are offered by the proponents of **neoliberal** austerity as the solution to social problems in large part caused by their own policies of abandonment and dispossession. Likewise, both human trafficking legislation[100] and schemes for offender rehabilitation position punishment as a kind of care for the person being criminalised. In echoes of Britain's imperial self-image as a crusading force for humanitarian good, it is in the name of safety and security that these institutions build spaces in which individuals are incarcerated and exposed to systematic violence and neglect.

This **paternalistic** brutality is, of course, not random but targeted at particular classed and racialised groups. One might think that the racist impact of these systems is simply a hangover from a long-ago time when racist dehumanisation had the economic function of legitimising slavery and colonial extraction. This view might suggest that the institutional racism of the police force and the immigration system could be and should be eradicated through reorganisation, training and other reforms. However, we would respond by showing how the continued differential violence of prisons, police and border enforcement has clear, and often intended, political, social and economic functions. As Stuart Hall reminds us, the **carceral** violence of the state is not merely discriminatory, it is central to the social reproduction of race and class.[101] Take conditional visa programs and the criminalisation of undocumented migration (as laid out in Shahvisi's piece in this collection). Now think about the criminalisation of stealing and strikes. Through these examples, we see how the legal violence of the state shapes the possibilities of acting against exploitative and oppressive conditions, and therefore *constitutes* the economic and political contexts in which we live. In short, the state depends on policing, detaining, and deporting people to re-secure a '**disciplinary**, capitalist and racially stratified society'.[102]

The final way both borders and policing help to maintain racial capitalism is by shaping **hegemonic** geographies of violence. In different ways, they both construct ideological boundaries between spaces that work to determine what violence is hidden and what violence is seen, what kind of violence is deemed **legitimate** and what kind requires disciplinary intervention. Prisons are imagined as a necessary response to harm in the community. But the violence within the prison, including the normalised, systematic, orderly harm needed to maintain it, is made invisible. At a different scale, border enforcement similarly constructs a geographical imaginary in which the UK is under constant threat from migrant **others** that insulates the post-imperial

British state from responsibility for global wealth and health apartheid.[103]

DISRUPTIVE SOLIDARITY

By drawing attention to similarities in their historical emergence, social function and coercive techniques, we have argued that critiques of border enforcement must extend to domestic policing and prisons. In this last section, we explain why solidifying these connections in migrant rights organising is a necessary strategic manoeuvre. This is important because regimes of criminal punishment and border enforcement subject social groups to surveillance and subjugation in ways that make it difficult to create and sustain connections of solidarity between prisoners, detainees, migrants, and allies.

Immigration and 'criminal justice' regimes assert that the individuals they target have personal deficiencies that cause their exposure to state violence. One way of protecting a person from state violence is by showing that they are different from the rest: that they are individually innocent or deserving of belonging.[104] This means that resistance is often limited to arguing that someone is either *not criminal* or *not foreign*. In doing so, our collective resistance to the state's ever-changing codification of criminality and foreignness gets **depoliticised**.

When the state creates categories of legitimate and illegitimate migrants, or when it differentiates between a criminal and a law-abiding citizen, these terms seem objective. But policing brings those categories to life, brings those words into lives, into homes, out of homes and into cells. And in so doing, they become flexible and expansive. They morph into 'folk devil' tropes that demonise individuals and groups, rendering them outside the boundaries of acceptable public sympathy, and in the case of supposed terrorism suspects, beyond the reach of civil and human rights.[105]

Systems of coercion and control are designed to separate those targeted by state violence from their communities and allies. Yet, this differentiating and sorting between different groups of detained people is sometimes mirrored in movements that work for migrant rights. Social movements make moral distinctions between asylum seekers and economic migrants, and between detainees and prisoners. Documentaries such as the *Undercover: Britain's Immigration Secrets* exposé of Brook House Detention Centre have brought the brutal realities of immigration detention to ever wider audiences, and yet their storytelling has earnestly reproduced this pervasive **binary** between 'foreign criminals' and 'regular' migrants.[106] Replicating these kinds of distinctions in our own everyday lives and social movements is never going to stop more people being torn from their homes, families, communities, and thrown into detention and towards deportation. The state is well-resourced to legislate ever new definitions of criminal activity and even more punitive responses.

Instead of claiming that the criminalisation of migration is some aberrant form of criminalisation, our movements need to recognise that it is in fact an exemplary case that highlights the problems with criminalisation *tout court*. If our social movements can come together to refuse the political distinctions between border enforcement and the police, we can be open to relationships of solidarity and the spaces of shared learning that are necessary for the long work of remaking a world without borders, prisons and police.

———

Tom Kemp organises with Detained Voices, SOAS Detainee Support and Abolitionist Futures. He is also a researcher at Nottingham Law School, writing about the law and politics of immigration detention and policing and the theory-making and knowledge practices of activist movements that engage with and oppose systems of incarceration.

Phe Amis has organised with and been educated by the Unity Centre Glasgow, LGBT Unity Glasgow and the End Deportations campaign. Phe is a history PhD student at Goldsmiths researching 'How the Home Office does history' and the colonial mobility regimes that have shaped the form and culture of Home Office deportation policy-making since 1881.

Freedom of
Protest,
Public Order
& the Law

DEFENDING THE 'LIBERAL-DEMOCRATIC ORDER'

THE STRATEGIC-POLITICAL LOGIC OF COUNTER-SUBVERSION

Connor Woodman

———————

When it comes to [...] the work that the government is doing, and has done for a considerable period of time – we are constantly looking at individuals, groups. That's right and that's proper.

Priti Patel, UK Home Secretary[107]

I n January 2020, a UK Counter Terrorism Policing document surfaced listing dozens of political organisations – including Greenpeace, Extinction Rebellion and the Stop the War Coalition – as potential 'extremists', worthy of inclusion under the **Prevent strategy**.[108] A local error, the police initially insisted – even though the document was circulated to several government departments, nearly two dozen local councils, five police forces and Counter Terrorism Policing headquarters.[109]

A similar document, circulated widely across the national public sector, emerged soon after, putting paid to the idea that this was the unauthorised activity of a lone police force.[110] Clearly, large parts of the state consider it 'right' and 'proper', as Priti Patel put it, that swathes of progressive political organisations come under the watchful eye of the state's anti-terrorism and counter-extremism branches.

How should this incident be interpreted? As a rogue aberration, bureaucratic zeal gone awry? As a laughable waste of police resources? Or as inexplicable 'nonsense', as then Labour leadership contender Lisa Nandy put it?[111]

None of these responses – common across the political spectrum, and even from those subject to police and intelligence spying – get at the common strategic-political logic of political surveillance, the deep explanation for why these revelations and scandals appear again and again in UK history. The British 2010s were punctuated with political surveillance scandals: from the ongoing 'Spycops' abuses, exposed in 2010 (concerning the roughly 150 police officers deployed undercover into British political organisations since 1968),[112] to the 2014 revelation of GCHQ's 'Joint Threat Research Intelligence Group',[113] to the Metropolitan Police's confirmation in 2018 that they had collaborated with the Consulting Association to blacklist construction workers active in trade unions.[114] Few political commentators take a historical view, instead treating each new revelation as a *sui generis* phenomenon.

In fact, the practices and units exposed throughout the 2010s are only the most recent instantiations of a specialised **counter-subversion apparatus** that stretches back, at least, to the establishment of the Metropolitan Police Special Branch in the 1880s. Since then, the British state has crafted dozens of organisations, units and special committees dedicated to monitoring, infiltrating and undermining, in the main, left-wing political groups. MI5 and Special Branch have constituted the beating heart of this apparatus. Viewed in the context of two centuries of British policing practice, the latest (January 2020) exposure comes as no great shock. The unceasing persistence of these counter-subversion programmes, which continue relatively untouched across political administrations of all hues, suggests they have some kind of functional utility for the state.

This functionality, occasionally alluded to in mainstream intelligence scholarship but rarely unpacked,[115] it is the task of **analysis** to unravel – to uncover the *strategic-political logic* of this state apparatus of counter-subversion. We can do this at three levels: 1) the counter-subversion system's own explicit self-justification; 2) the underlying functional role of the apparatus in maintaining a broader social order; and 3) the internal logic of the apparatus, the principles and practices through which it performs its functional role.

The first level is concerned with the formal constitutional role and justificatory **discourse** of the secret state, which, whilst ladled with the grease of **ideology,** can nonetheless unveil certain key features of the system's operation. The second is concerned with the external factors that motivate the existence of counter-subversion, the broader 'social structures' analysed by Georg Rusche and Otto Kirchheimer that the apparatus is functional in maintaining.[116] Beyond this 'general background', the third level must, as Michel Foucault wrote, 'bring out' the 'precise function' of the counter-subversion apparatus.[117] We must bring out the internal logic by which the apparatus helps maintain the current order.

LEVEL 1: COUNTER-SUBVERSION'S SELF-JUSTIFICATION

In 2019, shortly before Extinction Rebellion (XR) was named on the Counter Terrorism Policing document, Policy Exchange – the right-wing think tank with deep connections to the Conservative Party – published a report on XR, 'Extremism Rebellion'.[118] The report, a 72-page examination of the anti-systemic and often Leftist orientation of many of the key activists involved in XR, contained a preface by Richard Walton, former head of the Metropolitan Police Counter Terrorism Command (into which Special Branch was amalgamated in 2006). In the foreword Walton, previously distinguished for his involvement in the undercover infiltration of the family justice campaign of murdered Black teenager Stephen Lawrence in the 1990s,[119] offers an exemplary statement of the counter-subversion apparatus's own self-conception.

Walton denounces the 'subversive agenda' of the leading inner circles of XR as one 'rooted in the political extremism of anarchism, eco-socialism and radical anti-capitalist environmentalism'.[120] Their tactics '[condone] the breakdown of the rule of law', eventually leading to the 'breakdown of democracy and the state'. XR is, he writes, 'an extremist organisation whose methods need to be confronted and challenged […] by Ministers and politicians, the Commission for Countering Extremism, police and the general public'. XR must, Walton counsels, '[acknowledge] the liberal-democratic order' rather than 'encouraging mass law-breaking'.[121]

As Walton's preface illustrates, the upper echelons of the British state view their mission as, in part, preserving a particular social order – what Walton calls the 'liberal-democratic order'. The core of the official definition of subversion, retained across decades of minor adjustments, describes as subversive those political actions which 'threaten the safety or well-being of the State and are intended to undermine or overthrow Parliamentary democracy by political, industrial or violent means'.[122] MI5 still notes 'counter-subversion' as one of its statutory roles.[123]

The list of individuals and organisations targeted under this definition of subversion includes mass movements like the Campaign for Nuclear Disarmament and the Vietnam Solidarity Campaign, pressure groups like Greenpeace, mass trade unions and smaller political organisations. The 'democracy' the state pledges to defend does not refer to the engagement of a mass of people in shaping political life, but to the *particular instantiation* of (allegedly) democratic procedures in the British constitution. Forms of democratic practice that go beyond these narrow limits are deemed unacceptable, an undermining of democracy rather than its fuller expression. What is being protected is the *liberal-democratic order* referred to by Walton. This **liberalism**, dominant in Britain for at least two centuries, comprises, at its core, the interlacing of the capitalist economic system and the Westminster parliamentary system: respect for private property rights and a carefully delimited scope of individual political expression. According to one informed scholar, MI5's official list of potential targets to be defended from subversion included, as of 2009, 'the Anglo-Saxon model of capitalism'.[124] In short, the counter-subversion apparatus views its role as defending the prevailing politico-socio-economic system of the UK.

LEVEL 2: COUNTER-SUBVERSION'S FUNCTIONAL ROLE

While the explicit constitutional definitions and pronouncements of the secret state go some way to revealing the functional role of counter-subversion, remaining at that level risks taking the state's words at face value and missing underlying functions that may be operating beyond the stated (or even conscious) intentions of the apparatus's individual actors.

To illustrate the point, it is clear that many individuals and groups targeted by the apparatus cannot be considered, at face value, to come under the definition of 'subversive', to pose a serious threat to 'Parliamentary democracy'. MPs who seek only to engage in parliamentary procedures or to form a government, for example, have been explicit targets of the counter-subversion apparatus.[125] Many target groups have been fully signed up to the 'liberal-democratic order' – say, the National Council for Civil Liberties (now Liberty) – or were largely unconcerned with broader political or revolutionary change – the Anti-Apartheid Movement, for example.

Why, then, have such groups and individuals, apparently unsuitable candidates according to counter-subversion's self-professed aim, so consistently wound up the object of its gaze? Is there a common denominator underlying the target groups that could explain why they are of interest to the secret state?

A historical survey of the target groups, which I have undertaken elsewhere,[126] suggests that there is such a common denominator. In general, the groups caught in the surveillance and infiltration net, whether revolutionary or not, exhibited some form of what political philosophers Lorna Finlayson and Koshka Duff call 'deep dissent': 'dissent that seriously or fundamentally challenges the existing apportionment of wealth and power in society'.[127] More specifically, the groups sought to weaken, undermine or destroy one or more of the set of **hierarchical** social relations that order the British polity: social relations of class, race, gender, **imperialism** and **heteronormative** sexuality. The counter-subversion apparatus's *function* is to *defend* and even, in part, *constitute* these hierarchical social relations.[128]

To illustrate, take two examples from radically different historical moments.

The Legitimation League: In the late 19th century, the Legitimation League campaigned to remove the stigma from children born out of wedlock. The League drew the attention of Special Branch, which infiltrated and destroyed it from within in 1898. In the words of the Branch officer who penetrated the League, the secret state set out to 'kill a growing evil in the shape of a vigorous campaign of free love and Anarchism'.[129] The threat the League posed was not obviously one to 'Parliamentary democracy' or the 'safety of the State'; the League threatened certain hierarchical social relations, in this instance the structure of the late Victorian family. Since these **patriarchal** gender relations were defended and, in part, created by the state, political opposition to the relations had to be infiltrated and destroyed.

Family justice campaigns: The late 20th century UK witnessed the emergence of campaigns for justice for Black people and others killed by police or police-facilitated racist gangs. These 'family justice campaigns' have been routinely infiltrated, spied upon and subject to dark propaganda by police counter-subversion units. The campaign for justice for Stephen Lawrence, murdered by a White gang in 1993, for example, was infiltrated by the Metropolitan Police Special Demonstration Squad. Dwayne Brookes, one of Stephen's closest friends and there the night of his murder, was monitored with the explicit purpose of finding 'dirt' capable of undermining his credibility as a witness, according to the police officer who was ordered to carry out the operation.[130] On one level, these operations were simply attempts to protect the reputation of the police, challenged by accusations that they either deliberately killed people of colour or failed to properly investigate racist murders. But on a deeper level, these operations were attempts to defend the hierarchical social relations of race that are riven through British social life. Part of *what it means* to be subject to racism, or even to be Black in the UK, is to experience police harassment and violence.[131] These undercover infiltrations into Black justice campaigns undermined attempts to challenge the UK's racial order, and partly *constituted* that order through the meting out of racist treatment.

These hierarchical social relations are intrinsic to the liberal-democratic capitalist order, the order the counter-subversion apparatus is constitutionally mandated – and its functionaries often personally committed – to defend. Only, the ideological account liberalism gives of itself contains no recognition of its role in generating such social schisms. In fact, part of how liberal capitalism generates the huge cleavages of race, class and gender is precisely by concealing their existence beneath the **formal equality** of the market and law. Thus, the apparatus's own self-justification and legislated role contains no reference to the maintenance of these hierarchical social relations – rather, it is merely concerned with upholding 'parliamentary democracy', the 'rule of law', and abstract legal rights, such as the right of businesses to open and operate in the face of **hard pickets.**

This account provides a broad framework for analysing the function of the counter-subversion apparatus in the context of the wider social structure.

LEVEL 3: COUNTER-SUBVERSION'S PRINCIPLES OF OPERATION

The final level concerns the principles of operation by which the counter-subversion system carries out its function of monitoring, infiltrating and undermining deep dissent. Several non-exhaustive principles are outlined here:

A) *Principle of total political coverage*

One curious feature of the history of counter-subversion, a feature that invites reactions of ridicule, is the seemingly insignificant nature of some of the groupuscules targeted. From a 12-strong, all-women Maoist reading group to the Clandestine Insurgent Rebel Clown Army, some of the groups infiltrated by the Special Demonstration Squad and National Public Order Intelligence Unit appeared to pose little threat to anything – least of all to the foundations of the social order.

A central reason why such tiny groups are often surveilled and infiltrated can be found in the writings of Basil Thomson, the leading British counter-subversion officer in the tumultuous period of unrest following World War I. As he wrote in his memoirs, elites ought not to 'forget what determined minorities can do with an irresolute mass. A single fox will clear out a hen-roost while it is cackling its indignation to the skies'.[132] In Thomson's suggestive metaphor, 'Subversive societies are like the geysers in a volcanic field. After preliminary gurgling they sprout forth masses of boiling mud and then subside, while another chasm forms at a distance and becomes suddenly active'.[133] Because the state cannot know in advance which groups will become mass movements or disciplined cadre organisations – and hence threats to the prevailing order – all nascent groups must be monitored to check their potential growth and purchase amongst the population.[134] This principle puts the state in the driver's seat of social change, ready to run down any mass or revolutionary upsurge like a deer in the headlights.

As far as technical and resource restrictions allow, a **totalising** gaze should be directed at the political field. Social challenges and unrest that might be missed when focusing upon one area can be captured in the broader picture. In the words of the Advocate General of the colonial Dutch East Indies in 1919, empirical materials 'need to be pieced out, brought together, sorted out, and ordered [...] in order to know with more certainty than now how extensive a revolutionary drive of various associations has become'.[135]

Thus, MI5 classified up to 50,000 UK citizens as potential 'subversives' in the 1980s,[136] Special Branch recorded the details of possibly over one million individuals,[137] and the Special Demonstration Squad infiltrated dozens of Left-leaning political groups for over 50 years.

B) *Principle of active disruption*

Sometimes the secret state moves from intelligence collection to active intervention. This can be necessary to check the advance of a substantial organisation or movement: to protect a particular set of social relations under political strain, defend the interests of a particular power centre (say, the police or a favoured corporation under attack by a political campaign), or for the purposes of counter-revolution. Disruption operations can range from the subtle undermining of **direct actions** to the deployment of full-blown *agents provocateurs*.[138]

The instances in the historical record are numerous. Two of the most significant concern the active infiltration and undermining of the Communist Party of Great Britain,[139] at its height in the 1940s reaching around 50,000 members, and the infiltration and effective destruction of the National Union of Mineworkers in the 1980s and 1990s, documented in great detail by Seamus Milne.[140] Both operations had far-reaching effects on the course of British political history and the avenues available for dissent against the 'liberal-democratic order' defended by Watson. Nonetheless, this principle has as its limit other principles of operation, not least the need to maintain secrecy and to ensure effective *monitoring* of political threats. It is clear that most undercover operations are not designed to secure prosecutions or even to actively disrupt, but to gather information.[141]

C) *Principle of the 'chilling effect'*

Undercover infiltration and ubiquitous surveillance have the useful effect of generating paranoia within the ranks of political organisations. New recruits are the object of harsh suspicion, and even the closest romantic ties between individuals can carry a cloud of doubt over their veracity. As Mark Kennedy, a former officer who spent around nine years infiltrating the British environmental movement, put it following his uncovering: 'the police have had a result by me being exposed [...] the paranoia levels I would imagine within the activist community have probably gone through the roof'.[142] This weakens the efficacy of political organising and its potential threat to dominant social relations.

This principle is somewhat diffuse. It is unclear to what extent it operates as a conscious aim of the counter-subversion apparatus, which undertakes extensive precautions to prevent its operations and operatives from becoming known to its targets.[143] Secondly, the principle operates in part through the targets themselves, who sometimes project a penumbra of paranoia over an entire population of actual or potential supporters. In classic Foucauldian terms, this chilling effect, whilst functioning as part of a clearly 'decipherable' structure of power, 'comes from below'.[144]

D) *Principle of secrecy*

Perhaps most obviously, counter-subversion operations require secrecy in order to avoid both effective counter-surveillance measures by the targets, and any potential public outcry about their extensive use.

This principle is, however, in tension with the principle of disruption. The more actively the counter-subversion apparatus intervenes in the political field, the more its vapours will be discoverable to the discerning eye. This tension is the source of many political surveillance scandals: instances where the state declined to intervene in a drastic political action in order to protect its intelligence sources,[145] or when interventionist hubris led to exposure. The balancing act between secrecy and intervention depends on how well intervention can be concealed, how well a mysterious intervention will produce the useful corollary of the chilling effect, and how much of a threat is posed by bubbling political unrest.

CONCLUSION

In sum, a broad historical view of political surveillance and infiltration allows us to understand its role as a tool in a political power struggle. The state, to a large extent, defends and constitutes hierarchical social relations: cleavages of race, class and gender, which pulsate through the social body to the rhythms of domination and exploitation. These cleavages generate political resistance, forms of struggle intended to weaken or destroy these social relations and institute a more equal and emancipated order. The counter-subversion apparatus is a key coercive force working to contain these threats to the current order.

Rather than retreat into paranoia and obsessive counter-surveillance measures, those who wish to bring about social change must do two things. First, we must struggle to dismantle the laws and policies that facilitate the tactics and existence of the counter-subversion apparatus, with a horizon towards total *abolition* of the apparatus. Second, and in the process of the first, we must build a mass movement broad, popular and strong enough to reduce the power of counter-subversion's tricks. We must, in short, generalise subversion beyond the control of the powers that be.

Connor Woodman is an independent writer and researcher and the author of the 'Spycops in Context' papers published by the Centre for Crime and Justice Studies. He has had the dubious honour of being discussed by BP's Intelligence, Security and Crisis Management section while studying politics, philosophy, economics and history at the University of Warwick.

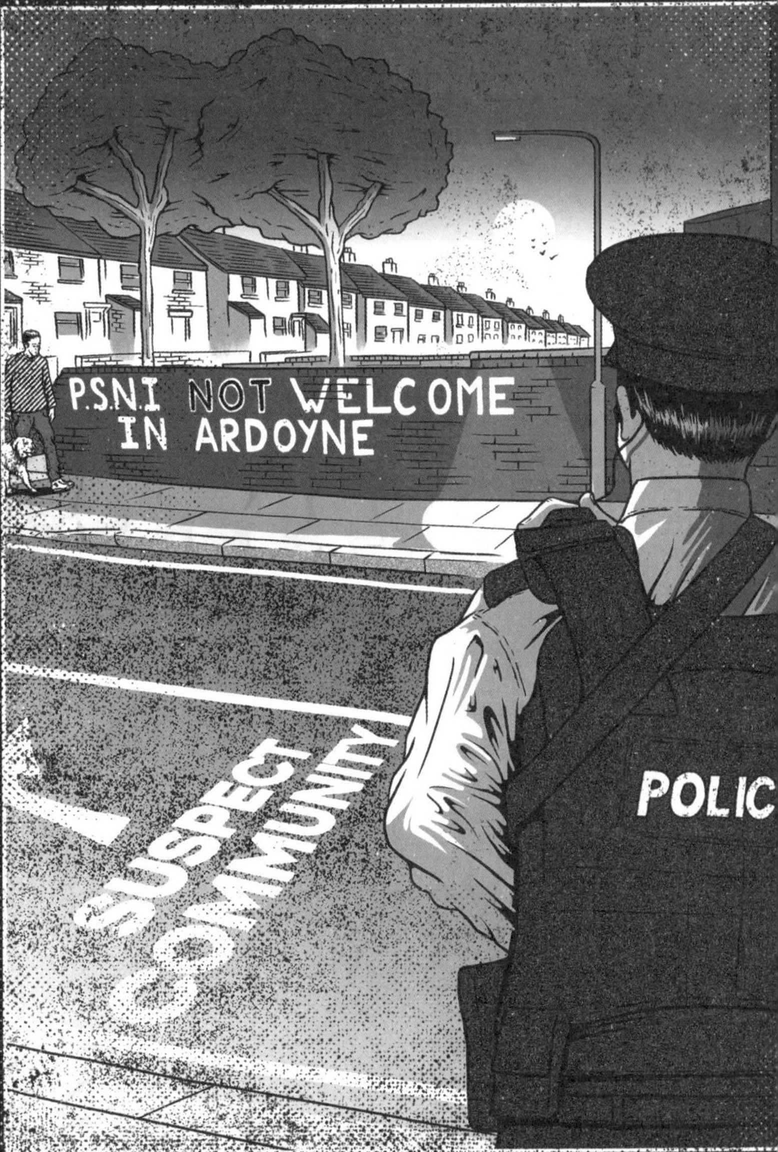
P.S.N.I NOT WELCOME
IN ARDOYNE
SUSPECT
COMMUNITY
POLIC

FROM THE COLONY TO THE METROPOLE
RACE, POLICING AND THE COLONIAL BOOMERANG

Tanzil Chowdhury

The colonies were productive spaces – not just in terms of the profits that were extracted back to the **imperial** centre (the metropole) through **expropriated** land and exploited or enslaved labour, but also the forms of governance that were enacted and **operationalised** in these 'recalcitrant colonies' and exported back to the centre. The oscillating movement, in which practices in the 'laboratory of the colonies' moved into the metropole, also went back 'throughout the world as part of the **neo-colonial** expansion of commercial interests'.[146]

The violence of the imperial project is not a mere historical curiosity, nor did it only take place in a 'distant land'; it shaped and continues to shape the technologies of British state violence today. This short piece aims to locate contemporary policing in the UK as part of this multi-directional movement – the '**colonial boomerang**' – of policing cultures and techniques that moved between the colony and the metropole. In his *Discourse on Colonialism*, Aimé Césaire famously wrote how Nazism emerged not as a 'mass psychosis of the German nation' but from 'the fact that he [Hitler] applied to Europe colonialist procedures which until then had been reserved exclusively for the Arabs of Algeria, the "coolies" of India, and the n***ers of Africa'.[147] Indeed, writing at the start of the war, George Padmore said that the colonies were 'the breeding ground for the type of fascist mentality which is being let loose in Europe today'.[148] This chapter attempts to draw lines of continuity and connection between contemporary policing and that of a much more imperial vintage.

Critical histories of policing, in particular looking at the formation of the Metropolitan Police in the UK, relate 'the rise of professional policing to the conjunctural crisis of early capitalism' and the desire of the state to **pacify** an emergent industrial working class.[149] While largely correct, such accounts suffer from a provincialisation of the UK and thus the erasure of its imperial entanglements – including its police force – with the rest of the world. Indeed, 'the traditional histories miss one major salient feature of the policing of early nineteenth century Britain: its growing importance as an imperial power'.[150] Governance in the colonies, protectorates, mandates, dominions across Asia, Africa, the Americas and the Middle East had a contagion effect[151] whereby policing in the UK not just constituted policing in the colonies but was also constituted by it.

The UK's oldest white settler colony of "Northern Ireland",[152] arguably the dawn of Great Britain's 'empire of capital',[153] provided an important space for logistical and strategic experimentation with the policing of dissent and anti-colonial resistance (though 'crime reduction' was the useful **ideological** cover that rationalised such practices). This was then transported back into and normalised in the UK, especially in its policing of **racialised** communities. The Royal Irish Constabulary (and then the Royal Ulster Constabulary) were a heavily **militarised** police force that were central to protecting British interests in the Irish War of Independence in 1921. In order to manufacture consent, particularly on the British mainland, the RIC engaged in a concerted propaganda campaign against the indigenous Irish population. In a move that would then become embedded within the policing culture in "Northern Ireland", the RIC framed the indigenous peoples as a perpetual threat to British imperial interests. This was no different to the productions of racial regimes, techniques and practices of imperialism elsewhere. As Patrick Wolfe writes, when colonisers are threatened with the requirement to share social space, 'racialisation' describes the process in which the colonisers impose classificatory grids on local populations to co-ordinate particular ends. Race is colonialism speaking.[154] **Orientalisation** – the process whereby imperial states frame other societies in a way that inferiorises them, and **legitimates** domination, restructuring, and having authority over them[155] – was key here. The Irish's 'wild shamrock manners' needed to be policed and placated.[156] It should come as little surprise that the founder of the Metropolitan Police, also the Chief Secretary to Ireland, Sir Robert Peel once described the Irish and their 'natural predilection for outrage and a lawless life' as something he thought couldn't be controlled. Irish communities were identified as what Paddy Hillyard famously referred to as 'suspect communities'[157] and this would legitimate the use of **exceptional powers** put in place by the state to police and dominate them.

While policing cultures and techniques in white settler colonies (e.g. Australia, the US, Canada, South Africa, New Zealand) were typically civilian in nature, "Northern Ireland" was an important exception. Policing here was more in the rhythm of policing in colonies of racialised populations (i.e. non-settler colonies). These were often paramilitary in their operationalisation, blurring the functions between the police and the army.[158] The RUC's militarism meant that they were typically 'under direct political control, barracked, generally armed, and often military or quasi military in nature, with officers having recourse to wide emergency and "special" legal powers'.[159] Hillyard described how the RUCs militarisation was evidence that the colony was a testing ground for the policing of civil unrest and public disorder.[160] Also central to the militarised policing strategy was intelligence gathering, an innovative tactic that was then transplanted to the British Raj in setting up the Calcutta Special Branch.

The 'boomerang effect' of policing in "Northern Ireland" was to have a direct consequence in the UK. Paul Gilroy wrote how:

> the continuing war in the six counties of Northern Ireland has had profound effects on the police service on the mainland. These go beyond the simple but important idea that operational techniques, methods of surveillance and even structures of criminal justice refined in that experience are being progressively implemented in Britain.[161]

The historical record substantiates Gilroy's claim. Many senior officers visited "Northern Ireland" to learn from the 'successes' in riot control.[162] Arthur Wellesley (the 1st Duke of Wellington), Sir Robert Peel and Sir Henry Goulborn, who are considered the key progenitors in drafting the legislation that helped set up the London Metropolitan Police in 1829, had all served as Chief Secretary in Ireland too. Sir Kenneth Newman, formerly an officer in the British Mandate of Palestine and then Chief Constable of the RUC during the height of 'The Troubles' would then become the Commissioner of the Metropolitan Police in 1982. Sir Robert Mark, who was the Met's Commissioner during the beginning of 'The Troubles', famously said that 'some of the tactics adopted by the London police, and later by other forces, were those developed and used by the Army and the RUC [Special Patrol Groups] in Northern Ireland'. What policing in "Northern Ireland" brought to the UK was a militarisation in the practice and operationalisation of policing in urban areas, rationalised through an orientalising **discourse** directed against **diaspora** populations (i.e. people who have been dispersed/dispelled from their indigenous territories).

We might describe this boomerang effect as constituting what Stephen Green calls the 'new military urbanism'. If, as Wolfe writes, this racialisation emerges out of the colonisers' fear of having to share social space with an indigenous population, then the new military urbanism 'renders cities' communal and private spaces, as well as their infrastructure – along with their civilian populations – a source of targets and threats'.[163] Intersecting with these militarist overtones – as we saw in the colonies – are processes of race-making between the former imperial metropole and diaspora populations *within* the UK mainland. Indeed, Green writes how:

> contemporary resurgence in the importation of typically colonial tropes and techniques into the management and development of cities in the metropolitan core [...] stress [...] explicitly colonial strategies and techniques amonst nation states [...] in the contemporary 'post-colonial period' not just in the deployment of troops for foreign intervention but their diffusion and imitation through the securitization of Western urban life.[164]

Herein lies the transplantation from the colony of "Northern Ireland" to the UK mainland and the durability of colonial policing and racialisation today.

Intersecting with this contemporary iteration of colonial policing, military urbanism is imbued with an 'inner city orientalism' that similarly constructs diaspora communities and communities of colour from Moss Side to Brixton, Chapel Town to Tottenham as 'gangsters' or 'terrorists'.[165] Again, Gilroy's writing on the connections between national decline and race is instructive here. He explains how 'unified national culture articulated around the theme of legality and constitution' is alleged to have been violated by 'black criminality', illustrating how the disruption of obedience to law is part of the ubiquitous threat to British culture that blackness poses.[166] This internal orientalism is often articulated through panics, from 'mugging'[167] to the 'black party'[168] or the pervasiveness of 'knife-crime' and its alleged concomitancy with drill music. These provide new rationalities for a military urbanism in such communities. The 'low-intensity wars' of 'The Troubles' in "Northern Ireland" re-emerge through suspicionless stop and searches of Muslims at airports and the pre-emptive logics of the **Prevent programme** (a 'counter-terror' programme that is widely held to racially profile Muslims); or the intersection of the gangs matrix and 'joint enterprise laws that criminalise groups of young black men';[169] or the shoot to kill policies that have killed Jean Charles de Menezes, Azelle Rodney, Mark Duggan and Anthony Grainger; or the normalisation of armed police units patrolling areas with 'visible gun use',[170] the general increase in the number of armed officers,[171] and the increase and disproportionate use of tasers against Black and Asian communities.[172] In 2012, then Metropolitan Police Commissioner, Sir Bernard Hogan-Howe, tellingly described *Total Policing* (the Met's slogan at the time) as 'using all the powers we have, all the levers we can access, all the skills and capabilities of our people in a total war on crime'.[173]

Descriptions of European empires, even by their more critical chroniclers, tend to have one thing in common: all portray the imperial centres – *the metropoles* – as having an expansionary fanaticism and fervour to universalise Western modernity and/or the social relations of capital **accumulation**. The implication is that empire was something done to a well-crafted '**other**', a unilateral imposition of domination, submission and exploitation over previously flourishing civilisations. The reality, however, betrays this caricature of imperial social relations. A. Sivanandan's oft-quoted 'we are here because you were there' can be broadened to illustrate the point – not only to explain the presence of **Global South** diasporas (from the regions of Latin America, Asia, Africa, and Oceania) in the European metropolitan centres, but to reflect a truer sense of imperialism's boomerang effect, which included the cultural artefacts, social systems (including innovative policing techniques) and suchlike that ricocheted from the colonies back to the 'motherland'. Indeed, we continue to see the boomerang of 'police exchanges' between settler-colonial states like Israel and the US, for example.[174] This grand policing strategy directed against migrant, diaspora and communities of colour, focusses our attention on the police's proximity to the state and the enactment of state violence against those peoples. As with colonialism and its production of race that emerges out of a sharing of social space, techniques of race-making and policing are imported from the British state's former colonies to the spaces where those diasporas now live in the UK mainland. Policing today, therefore, is a war against the poor and racialised, a continuing application of lessons learned in the colonies of empire.

Tanzil Chowdhury is a founder of the Northern Police Monitoring Project, an independent, grassroots organisation working with communities and families facing police harassment, brutality and racism. He is also a lecturer in the School of Law at Queen Mary University of London, where he teaches and researches on law, war, empire and capital.

STATUES AND GANGS
FASCIST PANIC AND POLICING

Becka Hudson

'You're antifa! This is what antifa looks like. She's antifa!' So shouted a far-right demonstrator at a police officer in London, in June 2020.[175] The officer's cordon separated him and his fellow demonstrators from the mostly young, black counter-demonstrators nearby. This choice moment in Britain's white nationalist history occurred a week after the Black Lives Matter (BLM) uprising had resounded over the Atlantic and swelled into demonstrations across the UK – the largest anti-racist mobilisations in the country's history. This far-right rally gathered in response, purportedly to 'defend statues'. Initially called by premier neo-Nazi Tommy Robinson, the 'Democratic Football Lad's Alliance' (DFLA) and their allies from a constellation of far-right, nationalist and outright fascist groups were present. They were not racist, they insisted to reporters throughout the day, but rather incensed that last week the statue of Edward Colston, a man who had kidnapped, killed and enslaved 84,000 people from Africa and donated to the poor of England with some of the proceeds,[176] had been dumped in the Bristol harbour by BLM demonstrators. The London monument to Winston Churchill, wartime Prime Minister and architect of the Bengal famine,[177] too, had been daubed with the strapline 'WAS A RACIST' that day.

Seven days of media debate about etiquette and iconography ensued. A friend was asked to go on the BBC to discuss, as the producer made clear, not *whether* statues of men from 'our history' with 'views we might not agree with' should be taken down, but rather *how*. Weren't petitions preferable to protests? Criminal damage was surely not an appropriate vehicle for positive change, it being, after all, a crime. *Were they condoning criminality?* The course of the debate in the **liberal** press seemed to all but obscure what had first driven BLM demonstrators to take to the streets – racist police violence. Indeed, although at the protests police had gathered personal information from BLM demonstrators in legally dubious ways; a horse had trampled over and seriously injured one protester after police charged like cavalry on a group of unsuspecting young black people whom they had **kettled**; children as young as 12 had been arrested late at night; and police had held protesters, during a contagious disease epidemic, in tight cordons of hundreds until 2am – *their* conduct, their violence, their aggressive and repressive racism, was scarce mentioned.

For both a far right that accuses police of being 'antifa', and for liberal commentators terribly worried about crime, police are understood to exert force in order to uphold agreed-upon standards of conduct: to protect protesting citizens from fighting, property from being stolen, and statues from being dumped in rivers. I argue, however, that policing is being increasingly weaponised by far-right strategists who understand that the already existing racist brutality of liberal policing can be agitated to expand state violence against black, brown and migrant populations, and that perceived failures or insufficiencies in this violence may be leveraged to legitimise hard-right vigilantism in the form of racist attacks.

FASCIST PANIC AND THE POLICE

Largely absent from discussions about the conduct of BLM protests, the figure of the police returned to centre stage for the far-right's counter-mobilisations. Alongside the above demonstrator's accusation that police are 'antifa', the Met faced smoke flares, bottles, barriers, fireworks and punches thrown their way. Throughout the beer-saturated spree of racist chauvinism, demonstrators continually asked police: *where were you last week?* At least one crowd of several hundred demonstrators broke into song – 'Where the fuck was you last week?' – as police cordons held them back. The fascists were upset that cops had not defended the statues. But it was more than this. Previous defacements of those same statues at almost every mass demonstration in central London over the last decade had not solicited such a large, aggressive far-right response. They were upset more particularly that the police had not meted out appropriate discipline on the predominantly black protests for black lives. Then, tens of thousands filled the streets to condemn systematically racist, sometimes lethal, police violence, even as they were subjected to it; here, the far right were bussed in from across the country to say: this violence is *not enough*.

A number of liberal and centre-right commentators condemned far-right attacks on 'our police' while holding up their loutishness as an example of what an own-goal the march had been. They looked like thugs. Even Boris Johnson, a Prime Minister who has consistently refused to acknowledge or apologise for his own instances of gross racism, condemned the day's 'racist thuggery'[178] (on the sure footing that he had condemned BLM demonstrators' own 'thuggery' a week prior).[179] Certainly, the far right had shown themselves to be a disrespectful bunch. But were they there to be respectable? It is true they had gathered to affirm the titans of UK establishment history, enshrined in statues at its town centres: the slave traders, the genocide architects, the heroes of imperialist war. All in all, however, their tone was anti-establishment. It was vehemently anti-police. It was a show of force, a corrective to a perceived deficiency of police violence against black protest.

In the hours after, the state assembled its own correction. Until 2am that night, police stopped, searched and arrested scores of black people in central London. Many were simply walking in the area, unconnected with any protest. Within a day, the government had thrown more of its own weight into the debate. A new law would ensure that those found defacing war memorials would face ten years in prison. Though the charge of criminal damage already carries a maximum ten-year sentence, here was a new power specifically to discipline statue defacement. The state offered its settlement on the iconography debate: no more Churchills would be defaced without heavy penalties; there would be harsher disciplining of black protest. The monuments to the slavers, the genocide architects, the imperialist war heroes were now protected with penalties longer than the average sentence for rape.[180] Calls from the right, and from the far right on the street that day, were absorbed, formalised and bolstered into the state's own violence. Statue crime was now its own entity.

State abandonment and state violence are a couple. Police in the UK, the oldest police forces in the world, are born of imperialist violence and the liberal state's need to discipline members of its labouring class, particularly the under- and unemployed.[181] It is true that since the 1980s there has been a drastic expansion of policing in step with the '**neoliberal** turn'. Increased state capacity came to bloat prisons and police departments while restructuring elsewhere hollowed out support for citizens and scaled up privatisation.[182] But the abandonment/violence relationship goes farther back than this. For populations who have been consistently underserved, excluded from and stripped of resources – black and brown people living in the metropole, for example – a lack of resources and abundance of policing have long been the standard conditions of a life in the UK. This was the case even when the welfare state, whose erosion marks the start of the neoliberal turn,[183] was in its heyday. To be sure, no government in recent history or near imagined future would concede such a connection exists. But this historical baggage, the basis of policing's function, drives its shift (far-) rightwards and proves a sturdy launchpad for far-right demands on its conduct.

AN ANATOMY OF FAKE CRIME

The British public imagination remains replete with nightmares about **racialised** crime. This year, there are statue desecrators. In the 1980s, there were muggers.[184] There is always the figure of the thug.[185] The illegal immigrant. The terrorist. More recently, over the past decade, there have emerged particularly frightening types of gang: drill music-producing gangs escalating knife crime within inner cities and running 'county lines' of child drug dealers outside of them; and the 'Asian grooming gang', networks of Muslim South Asian men engaged in child sexual exploitation who target white girls. Each of these formations have congealed into public consciousness in as little as a few months through liberal media and political posturing. They are often then **reified** in policing infrastructure. Databases for suspected radicalised youth and gang members require remarkably low thresholds of proof to store an individual's data for further surveillance, injunctions restricting their movement and activity, conditions on immigration or citizenship status, access to essential services, or increased intrusion of violent policing – including home raids and repeated stop and search – into everyday life. The Metropolitan Police's Gangs Matrix, for example, stores the information of almost 4,000 people, 78% of whom are black, and the majority of whom – by the police's own estimation – pose no threat.[186]

It is perhaps worth a disclaimer that all crime is fake, in a sense. Demarcations of behaviour as illegal, and the differential ways in which criminal law and its enforcement operate in people's lives, are in constant flux. Notwithstanding the development of these categories over time, even as they rest as stable entities, they do not operate consistently. Murder, for example, often carries a life sentence for a woman who kills her abusive partner; for the police officer who orchestrated the fatal shooting of an innocent man in a tube station, however, there was merely promotion to head of the Metropolitan Police.[187] The formations of the mugger, thug, gang member or terrorist that haunt public imagination are woven together in this context. They stand out as particularly fraudulent because they so disingenuously link crime's demarcation, and its control, to race and its proxies – one's housing, name, local area, school, religion, migration status or 'culture'. Though the violent conditions that such categories can impose on the lives of those caught within them are devastatingly real, nothing about these linkages is authentic.

The far right is agitated about all of these formations. Indeed, some of the largest far-right-led demonstrations in recent years have congealed them into a rallying cry against a generalised spread of black and brown criminals. In winter 2018, the DFLA held a mass London protest against *'returning jihadists, [...] thousands of AWOL migrants, light sentences for paedophiles and an epidemic of gang and knife crime'.*[188] Central to their narration of why so many undisciplined criminals walk the streets are the police. Criminals are causing great harm to people, communities, towns and cities, to national security and to their conception of British cultural, racial and moral order because the police have failed. The mismanagement of gang and knife crime by the Metropolitan Police is chalked up to a soft touch and loss of control over the city, often attributed to a politically correct cautiousness on behalf of the city's Muslim mayor, Sadiq Khan. It is popular amongst far-right circles online, including mainstream far-right commentators such as Katie Hopkins, to nickname the city 'Londonistan' whenever another stabbing (that is, on the street, as opposed to any of the scores of fatal stabbings that occur in domestically violent settings) takes place. An Islamophobic slight against Khan himself, no doubt, and one indicating his perceived inability to control the black and brown residents of his city and their criminal violence. It is not a fringe view. President Donald Trump has regurgitated concern about Khan's out of control London and its knife crime problem.

On 'grooming gangs', meanwhile, the story goes that rife abuse went uninvestigated and covered up by local authorities and police for fear of being 'seen as racist'. Again, a desire for political correctness drove police to avoid investigating and prosecuting Asian men. This story entered wider public consciousness via a *Times* investigation that lifted the 'Asian grooming gangs' label from far-right literature and presented an equation of 'sexual violence against white girls with national security'.[189] Later commissioned reviews that went looking for evidence of these frightening and horrific networks found that in fact police had dismissed girls' stories with victim-blaming misogyny. Far from being concerned with political correctness, police told a number of survivors they were 'asking for it', 'risk fuelled' or 'prostituting [themselves]'.[190] This total refusal of care, protection or interest in justice for these women and girls was intensified by their class position. Many were in institutional care settings, almost all were working class. They were black, white and Asian – and were targeted by groups of white men too. Police dismissals were, and continue to be, particularly acute when victims are themselves Muslim.

FASCIST INVOCATIONS OF POLICE VIOLENCE

These formations of racialised criminals – the gang, the terror network, the Muslim paedophile, the statue desecrator – are galvanising the far right. Agitating around these issues has seen some of the largest far-right mobilisations in decades and has heavily shaped public opinion. On each of these criminal formations, the far right are demanding *more* from police. Far from opposing the law and order apparatus *per se,* they seek to expand and intensify their scope and use of force. Their rallies insist that policing, immigration enforcement and the prison apparatus are not bearing down heavily enough on these criminals, and by proxy the black and brown communities that harbour them. A cursory look at the DFLA's website or those of organisations like Britain First, their allies on the street that day, shows petitions demanding escalated state violence: more weapons for police; no benefits, housing or essential services for criminals; more prisons, longer prison sentences and fewer 'privileges' in prison; and bans, deportations and revocations of citizenship for migrants. Again, this is not on the fringes of our politics. Access to essential services, from NHS care to free school meals, has been cut off for migrants with no access to public funds.[191] Recent sentencing in child sexual exploitation cases saw Muslim men have their British citizenship revoked.[192] Black people who have lived in the UK since they were toddlers have been deported as 'foreign national offenders' after traffic violations or drug possession convictions.[193] Our youth offending institutions, though locking up far fewer young people in total than they were 10 years ago, are obscenely racially disproportionate: 28% of those incarcerated here are black, despite making up only 3% of the population.[194]

In some ways, the far right well understand what police do. Indeed, police get to enact a great deal of disciplinary violence on the criminals that haunt fascists' imaginations with apparent **legitimacy** and without consequence. Although, compared with Greece,[195] the Philippines[196] or the United States,[197] British police are not an institution well-infiltrated or in overt alliance with the far right, they are proving to be a fulcrum for their demands. Far-right derision and condemnation of police failures can effectively agitate for the police, whose violence is born of racist control, to enact further state surveillance, discipline and brutality against black and brown people and political opponents. When police fail to mete out adequate violence, far-right figures are able not only to agitate for further police repression but to legitimise their own vigilantism: if the police won't do it, who will? It is not incidental that alongside a growing and insurgent far-right movement in this country, we have an ongoing expansion of **carceral** capacity led by the British state. Bloated since the 1990s, there has been a continuous extension of activities categorised as criminal, of prison places, of police capacity, and of police access to – and powers over – people. Bolstered anew with tough law-and-order talk from the government since 2019, policing can only ever go rightwards. The far right well understand this. It is time we did too. Abolish them.

Becka Hudson is a PhD researcher at UCL and Birkbeck looking at the experience, impact and history of personality disorder diagnoses in the UK prison system and British empire. She is a founding organiser of a number of campaigns around criminal justice issues.

BLACK LIVES AND THE STATE OF DISTRACTION

Eddie Bruce-Jones

[T]he function, the very serious function of racism, is distraction. It keeps you from doing your work. It keeps you explaining over and over again, your reason for being. [...] And you don't have to do it anymore. [...] Where the mind dwells on changing the minds of racists is a very dank place. [...] Racial ignorance is a prison from which there is no escape because there're no doors. And there are old, old men and old, old women running institutions, governments, homes all over the world who need to believe in their racism and need to have the victims of racism concentrate all their creative abilities on them.

Toni Morrison[198]

Texas State Trooper: Okay, Ma'am. You okay?
Sandra Bland: I'm waiting on you. This is your job. I'm waiting on you...
Texas State Trooper: Oh, you seem very irritated.

Ten years ago, I lived in New York, and spent one Monday evening every fortnight teaching GED (General Educational Development) courses at the women's prison at Rikers Island Correctional Facility. The women were highly engaged students. To hear their stories, their setbacks, and their aspirations was a privilege. They handed me the heavy inertia of mass incarceration for a few hours at a time, giving me a chance to wrap my mind around its density — its *Americanness*. Of the 15 women in my course, one was white and many did not speak English as a first language. The months, and sometimes years, that these women endured, locked away on the island, had scrambled the lives of their loved ones. My courses were not meant to stop the shock wave caused by their absence, but I hoped they would dim its effect by preparing the women to return to daily life and to secure jobs. I always worried that by teaching those courses, I was polishing the doorknobs of the prison — **legitimating** the violence of incarceration by making it palatable.

My colleague Abena and I often rode the prison bus back to the Queensboro Plaza subway stop in silence. I never asked her how she felt. We would typically discuss the lesson, occasionally a story told by one of the women, but we never really checked in with one another emotionally. I was always empty, drained of every ounce of energy. The women were motivated to learn, but there was a pessimism that we were all fighting — a scandalous scepticism about the future. As far as work goes, the teaching was not transformative, although it probably built the confidence of the women, and perhaps gave them tools to progress in an employment environment invariably cold to those with prison records. However, the work certainly constituted a transgression. Not the reading comprehension exercises themselves, but the act of teaching and learning, there and then. There was a tacit acknowledgment that we were all convened in the education wing of the building to collectively reckon with a racial, **patriarchal**, **heterosexist** system of criminalization to which none of us, neither teachers nor students, was immune.

In the context of teaching and learning, each session, alongside and sometimes by way of grammar review, grappled with a different contour of power. It was not planned that way, but it is an inevitable part of communication between human beings to establish a connection, to inquire about certain gestures or levels of energy such as a frown or lethargy, to situate oneself and one's partner in the most basic of ways. I knew that the women at Rikers were giving me an education, and that some lessons would take years to process. On the bus across the water back to Queens, the nighttime pressed hard on my lungs. I watched the floodlights flicker and disappear over the bridge, a dark blanket swallowing the prison and everyone in it.

Rikers Island is the same prison in which a teenager named Kalief Browder was held for three years until his case was dismissed and he was released. Kalief killed himself earlier this year. The 22-year-old had experienced the worst phase of his life at Rikers and was unable to bounce back. I thought about the women I had met on the island when I read about Browder's death.

Today, #blacklivesmatter and notably #sayhername and #transblacklivesmatter have mobilized to struggle against police killings of black people and to highlight the invisibility of deaths of black women and trans people. They organize with a keen awareness that the movement to stop police shootings is part of a larger struggle against the everyday **structural violence** that defines the criminal justice system. Ruth Wilson Gilmore, in *Golden Gulag*, defines racism as the 'state-sanctioned or extralegal production and exploitation of group-differentiated vulnerability to premature death'.[199] In this view, the current movement aims to stop deaths, some spectacular and some mundane, some immediate and some delayed, but all premature.

The enforcement of criminal law against the police gestures to the legacy of slavery and racial subjugation that we seek to address, alongside individual incidents of violence. It is a gesture of historical reckoning. As the Equal Justice Initiative reminds us, the recent killings of unarmed black people are not recent as such, but rather they are legacies of the lynchings carried out in the Jim Crow era. Police enabled and participated in fatal violence against black people and others in an attempt to enforce a **white supremacist** patriarchy with state power. This was, and continues to be, **structural racism** in action, and it is central to the relationship between the US state and all who live within its domain.

After each death, I find myself mouthing a cumbersome chain of lawyerly words, hoping for ironclad prosecution and maximum sentences, to bring to justice those who have killed Rekia Boyd, Tamir Rice, Mike Brown, and numerous others. I hear myself invoking the heroic terror of the criminal justice system. I make no illusions that this will spackle the gaping fault of the United States' racial terrain. To digress for a moment, I also work on refugee law, and though I support and believe in refugee claims for securing better lives for individual applicants, these prosecutions seem to me much like the promise of refugee law to effect real change: vacant. The international refugee law system, while important to scores of individual claimants, represses a more meaningful commitment to free movement and serves to further stabilize and legitimize a system of border violence and geopolitical exploitation. Criminal prosecutions in these cases of police murder are (sometimes) offered as individual sanctions only after the harm has been done, and they do not seek to reduce the widening net of **carceral** politics. But then again, is this the time to abandon the use of criminal justice?

Patricia Williams in her seminal work *The Alchemy of Race and Rights* reminds us that while logics of rights are dangerously reliant on the fixtures of state domination, we do need legal protection, if only to maintain some basic room to breathe and exist.[200] So perhaps we need rights to deflect the point of the knife of systemic violence, even if it does not prevent us from catching the edge.

To some extent, relying primarily on criminal sanctions against aggressors suggests that we value the symbolic strength and coercive force of law. This seems a mocking compromise for, as it stands, we know the police and, by extension, the state is not equipped to protect us from itself. Not all of us, anyway. We use the law though we are terrified of it, contemptuous of its Janus face. We ask the police for what we need, hoping they will not kill us before we have finished stating our claims.

So how do we put on hold our **critiques** of the constant, structural violence of the criminal justice system, including the **prison industrial complex**, while attempting to ensure that the lives of people of color are protected? Is it only the force of criminal sanctions that will keep police from killing us, or must there be something more sustainable? And can that 'something more' wait until we begin to dismantle the prison of racism, or must the state's coercive violence be invoked now to prevent the everyday carnage that we experience at the hands of the police?

Toni Morrison suggests that we should consider the seriousness of distraction. She contends that distraction is the work of racism and that racism is like a prison, incarcerating its subscribers. Morrison describes the ritual of inquisition, whereby people of color are asked to validate their heritage and their authority to speak and create.

This idea of distraction, considering the constant, tireless negation of the authority of non-white people to produce knowledge, can easily be applied to the #blacklivesmatter context inasmuch as spectacular violence also serves to distract. It can reorient social thinking, and movement politics, around the tip of the blade rather than the long edge of the knife. Distraction conditions us to think reactively, defensively, about our own inclusion. It is in the words we use and the size of the continents on the maps in elementary schools. It is being asked whether our own degradation upsets us. Distraction is not the shine of a coin; often it is the glint of a blade.

For the purpose of illustrating the point of distraction, it is helpful to think of the officers who have killed unarmed black people as **agents** of the state, rather than merely as individuals. Of course these officers enjoy more protection as individuals precisely because they are agents of the state, but an additional concern with resting hopes on individual prosecutions is that they call upon the state to regulate its own behavior. While we can push for greater efficiency and procedural equality in the prosecution of individual officers, the more transformative potential of contemporary antiracist movements is on the level of systemic and structural change, a far more difficult endeavor.

Various groups are doing work to critically connect police killings with other forms of structural violence, such as the African American Policy Forum and its work on the overpolicing and educational exclusion of young black and

Latina women and girls. The voices of #blacktranslivesmatter have highlighted the extremely high proportion of trans women of color murdered in the United States. Importantly, this thought assemblage led by queer and trans people of color has consistently invested in a prison abolitionist approach, in which it links the structural violence produced by incarceration with that of racism, gender, and body norms, capitalism and **imperialism**. This **analytical** position, advanced by Reina Gossett, CeCe McDonald, Janetta Johnson, Miss Major, Dean Spade, Sarah Lamble, Angela Davis, and many others, suggests that prison abolitionist politics and practices occupy a central position in advancing the creative potential of broad-based social struggle.

Acknowledging the politics of prison abolition as a way to open ourselves to the possibility of transformative change affords us the space to ask: Who benefits from the prison system as we know it, and who stands to lose the most from its perpetuation?

Strategically, then, we must be in at least two places at once if we hope to transform the environment in which we live. We must be seen and heard by the state and by law, but we must also present another vision of what our connectedness looks like, another way of being together. Distraction makes racism and state violence seem like moving targets, difficult to critique amid the constant, shifty inquisition. But we cannot forget that it is not racism that is moving — it does not have the potential to move very much, and we know its techniques better than those imprisoned within it. We are the ones with the ability to move, to envision a different place. We have to spend a great deal of time outside the prison to be able to recognize ourselves if and when we find ourselves inside it, reproducing its structures and logics, especially when we are in the service of disassembling it from within.

It is difficult not to allow the metronome of police killings to set the pace for antiracist political struggle in the United States. While organizers are thinking ahead of reactive politics, the distraction of the prison of racism threatens constantly to blur our focus on the material prison, the carceral state. Morrison's point is that we should not allow our creativity to be curtailed. If, as she suggests, those of us who are not constrained by the prison of racism are free, then we should never relinquish our ability to stay in motion, to strategize around our positions and negotiate our creativity on our own terms.

Author's note: This piece was originally published on 21st September 2015 in the Los Angeles Review of Books.

Eddie Bruce-Jones is a legal academic and anthropologist based at Birkbeck, University of London. His research and writing focus on migration, racism, sexuality, colonialism, state violence and citizenship. He serves on the Board of Directors of the Institute of Race Relations and the UK Lesbian and Gay Immigration Group, and the advisory board of the Centre for Intersectional Justice in Berlin.

POLICE ABOLITION AND RADICAL DEMOCRACY

Daniel Loick

———————

'On the deposition of law with all the forces on which it depends as they depend on it, finally therefore the abolition of state power', writes Walter Benjamin in the final paragraph of his famous 1921 essay 'Critique of Violence', 'a new historical epoch is founded'.[201] The radicalism of what Benjamin envisions as 'a new historical epoch' is immediately obvious: a world without 'state power', hence a world without all the institutions of violence that seem to be so deeply anchored in our current social and political routines – the military, the police, the prison, the border. In this brief intervention, I want to reflect on what implications Benjamin's vision has for the project announced in the title of this volume: 'abolishing the police'. It is noteworthy that Benjamin does use the term 'abolition' with respect to state power (i.e. state-based institutions of violence such as the police), but he chooses another, quite unusual term with respect to the law, namely 'deposition' (in German: *Entsetzung*). *De-posing the law* means overcoming what is 'posited' in the law, i.e.

its **heteronomous**, **alienated** character. To describe the law as 'heteronomous' (which in general is the opposite of '**autonomous**', a term for self-rule or self-government) is to say that it is an oppressive power standing over and against those subject to its force, alien to them and beyond their control. Benjamin decidedly does not demand to overcome law as such, but to give it a radically different shape and status.

The notion of a 'deposed law', I suggest, can be meaningfully understood as the idea of a *law without violence*, or more specifically, a legal order without police. To make this claim plausible, I start by recounting some of the main arguments formulated by the social movement of police abolitionism. Not only have police abolitionists put forward radical **critiques** of the police and their **ideological** justifications, they have also presented convincing models to replace state-inflicted violence. These alternatives have been based on two main premises: first, the '**formal**' elements of democracy (such as elections) must be accompanied by '**material**' or social elements (such as equal access to education) if they are to be meaningful; and second, it is necessary to find new, community-based ways of establishing **intersubjective** accountability. While these are essential corrections to a **bourgeois** notion of democracy, I argue, they lack a specific enough conception of the political autonomy usually invested in the idea of democracy. In line with W.E.B. Du Bois' term 'abolition-democracy', I propose a radical democratic interpretation of the project of 'deposing the law': participation in radically inclusive processes of deliberation and decision-making can create the conditions for a non-violent social integration and thus render police and other forms of coercion superfluous. This idea, I believe, can best be explicated through a theoretical collaboration of abolitionism and radical democratic thought.

Abolitionism as a distinct strand of critical theory and radical political practice situates itself within the tradition of the 19th century movement to end slavery in the United States. Pointing out the continuity of the history of racism and **white supremacy** under the capitalist regime, abolitionists understand their contemporary struggles as necessary parts of a yet to be completed project of liberation. While most 20th century abolitionists have focused on pointing out the historic continuities from slavery to the current **Prison-Industrial-Complex** and worked towards ending the racist regime of mass incarceration, some groups and initiatives have also concentrated on the role of the police in maintaining an oppressive social order. Inspired already by the Black Power activism of the Black Panthers in the 1960s and 70s and re-emphasized by the recent Black Lives Matter movement, police abolitionists have not only formulated a fully-fledged and comprehensive critique of the police, but also discussed visions and strategies for a world without police.

Police abolitionists have pointed out at least three structural yet problematic features of modern policing:[202]

1. *Police undermine democracy.* Not only dictatorships and tyrannical regimes but also so-called '**liberal** democracies'

have proved incapable of limiting the role of the police to merely executing the rule of law, instead allowing them to pursue their own ends under the guise of legality. 'The assertion', Benjamin concludes in the 'Critique of Violence', 'that the ends of police violence are always identical or even connected to those of general law is entirely untrue'.[203] For Benjamin, the institution of the police compounds its official 'law-preserving' function irreducibly with its own 'law-positing' propensity: police create their own laws (to 'posit' meaning to set down, establish, or create). This tendency of the police to emancipate themselves from being the mere means to enforcing the law can take the form of police officers, police unions, or, especially dangerous, police commissioners intentionally pursuing their own (almost always: right wing) political goals that openly undermine the agenda of democratically elected officials (like in New York in 2014, where police ostentatiously turned their backs to the newly elected Mayor Bill de Blasio at public events). But it often occurs in the form of 'minor' or normalized extralegal harassment of minorities on an everyday basis. Police, in their day-to-day interactions, function as 'streetcorner politicians'[204] or 'street-level bureaucrats',[205] giving them both the authority and the opportunity to make far-reaching decisions on how to use the violent means the state has entrusted to them, thus structurally placing them at the margin between lawful and unlawful actions.[206]

2. *Police establish a differential regime of* **subjectivation**. Police form our psyche, our mentality, our habits, our behavior

– they make us into **subjects**. This subject-formation, however, does not mark us all the same. Everyday interactions with the police affect people in different, yet equally fundamental ways.[207] The police are not just a coercive institution, operating with external force, they also shape the ways people move in the world, their habits, expectations, their bodily and psychic experiences. Through practices such as raids and stop and search, police habitually address parts of the population (standardly people of color, poor people, homeless people, drug users, sex workers, trans and gender non-conforming people) as potential criminals, thus creating massive psycho-social suffering and continually undermining their standing as equal citizens of a democratic commonwealth. To another part of the population (usually white and affluent), police offer themselves as an instrument for the protection of material or symbolic property, allowing them an **affectively** anchored identification with the police perspective. This difference has a geographical component: in some areas, police act similarly to an occupation force,[208] while in others they help to create imaginary 'white spaces' freed from all elements perceived as dangerous.[209] This differentiation not only impedes the democratic ideal of equality, it also prevents and blocks mutual empathy or taking responsibility, more broadly speaking.

3. *Police create insecurity*. The creation of security for life and limb is one of most widely invoked justifications for the state's **monopoly on violence**. Yet, police continue to threaten precisely the good they are supposed to provide. Members of the police force are often recruited from masculinist milieus

in which harshness, violence and domineering behavior are commonplace and valorized as 'manly'. These tendencies are further cultivated during service and cannot be restrained to it (it's no coincidence that in the US, police officers are 2-4 times more likely to commit acts of domestic violence than the rest of the population).[210] Police appear as security risks especially for marginalized and disenfranchised groups such as people of color or poor people – who not only cannot count on the police to protect them against hate attacks and harassment but often experience police presence itself as a manifest threat to their safety, as the many horrific cases of police brutality and police killings prove. But even from the majority perspective, a police-based notion of security is not unproblematic. In public **discourse** (often fueled by racist stereotypes),[211] only some issues become legible as safety issues, while others – such as traffic safety, safety at the work place, social security, ecological safety etc. – are much less prominent. This thematic dominance of policeable issues leads to an increasing investment of public funds into **carceral** institutions and thus often to defunding welfare state institutions.[212] These cuts eventually accelerate processes of social disintegration, which then in turn express themselves in the form of a higher crime rate. In other words: strengthening the role of the police and other coercive institutions often weakens (social) security.

For these reasons, police abolitionists fight – as the name implies – for the abolition of the police. However, the term 'abolition' can easily mislead, as it primarily suggests a subtraction or a loss of something that currently exists.

In fact, the project of abolition sees itself as part of a broader social transformation that is much more about changing the background conditions that necessitate oppressive institutions: abolitionists insist that the process of abolition is as much about inventing new institutions as it is about abolishing the old ones.[213] Anti-police activism has focused on two main strategies for creating alternatives to state-inflicted violence: shifting the focus from criminal to social justice and finding new, non-carceral responses to interpersonal harm.

Already at the center of the Black Panthers' 'community defense' tactics was the idea that not state coercion but only a radical expansion of social participation would increase safety for the community and its members. Although the Black Panther Party (BPP) existed formally until 1982, its heyday was between the end of the 1960s and the beginning of the 1970s. In this period, the Panthers were successful in becoming a decisive social force in some of the major cities in the US. Often, this meant taking responsibility for the organization of some of the main elements of societal life: with the unfolding of actual political power, the Panthers found themselves in the position of having to organize the social cohesion of the community – a task traditionally ascribed to the state. The abolitionist practice of the Panthers had two parts that were sides of the same coin, one 'negative', one 'positive'. The negative part was about protecting the community from state violence, a mission that they mostly accomplished through armed cop-watching and patrols that helped to prevent harassment and police violence. With this tactic alone, the Panthers increased security for Black communities, eliminating an important risk factor for racist assaults. From the beginning, this negative aspect – negative in the sense that it was about challenging and overcoming an existing practice – was accompanied by a positive aspect: inventing and establishing new practices. The aim of these practices was most of all to enable community members to become part of social life in the first place. The Panthers initiated a variety of 'survival programs', such as free breakfasts for school children, providing for medical care, housing, and a range of educational activities.[214] With this approach, the Panthers were able to integrate a milieu that traditional Marxist thought had dismissed as counter-revolutionary **lumpenproletariat** – as a class of pauperized outcasts deprived of any historical **agency**.[215] This strategy further increased safety in the community in a number of ways: by providing a social infrastructure and attending to people's most basic needs, the Panthers not only erased some of the main causes for behavior that the state views as 'criminal', they also created opportunities for communication, exchange, and education, thus fostering a stronger community bond. In addition, the BPP recruited many members from traditional gang milieus and initiated and facilitated ceasefires and peace agreements between competing groups.

The second major abolitionist strategy to find alternatives to police-based solutions has been the struggle to overcome interpersonal violence, in particular violence against women. In this fight, concepts developed by feminists of color are at

POLICE ABOLITION AND RADICAL DEMOCRACY

the forefront. One of the main reasons is that women and LGBTQI people, as the groups most vulnerable to sexual, domestic, or intimate partner violence, have insisted on the urgency of taking their everyday experience seriously instead of subordinating it to other issues that the traditional Left considered to be more pressing, such as economic equality. At the same time, feminists of color in particular have not trusted the state to guarantee their safety, given the fact that incarceration has not only failed to protect vulnerable groups from **patriarchal** violence but has also invited additional state violence into their communities, reinforcing the patriarchal logic of masculinist protection.[216] In the case of interpersonal violence, the search for alternatives to police-based solutions has mostly been pursued under the banner of the concepts of *transformative justice* and *community accountability* (as Melanie Brazzell's chapter explains). At the core of these models is the idea of organizing collective support for survivors while at the same time looking for ways to help the abusive person to take responsibility without recourse to the violent state apparatus.[217]

These two strategies – creating new possibilities for social participation as well as for accountability and responsibility – are indeed important elements of an abolitionist process of social transformation. Both foster processes of *empowerment*, they help individuals and communities to liberate themselves from their status of being the *object* of social domination and to become the *subject* of their own histories. Not only were they able to provide at least piecemeal functional equivalents to state responsibilities, most of all the creation of safety, they have also worked to dismantle systemic oppression and thus helped to establish social conditions under which people can more fully identify with their social worlds. However, these strategies do not yet fully exhaust the original promise of the concept of abolitionism.

In his major work, *Black Reconstruction*, W.E.B Du Bois introduced the term 'abolition-democracy' to describe a particular historical force, namely the alliance of workers and small capitalists in the aftermath of the American Civil War, between 1860 and 1880.[218] The original aim of the movement was to position both capital and labor resolutely against slavery. The 'positive' and the 'negative' sides of the project of abolition are already formulated here: it is not enough to be released from the bond of slavery, it is also necessary to have the possibility to participate meaningfully in political self-government.[219] The movement therefore pressed for full citizenship rights for former slaves and their participation in actual political decision-making. The movement quickly realized that political power can only be properly exercised if it is complemented by economic power, leading it to question the very economic foundation of the US. Abolition was thus not about *integrating* former slaves into already existing structures, but about demanding a fundamental *reconfiguration* of these structures.[220] Many scholars since have taken up the term 'abolition democracy' to remind us of the unfulfilled desires and unmet demands associated with the movement. At the end of the 19th century, instead of completing the process of Black liberation, an alliance of white workers and white capital counteracted the promise of the reconstruction era and was able to install a system of racial and economic oppression and disenfranchisement that continues to this day, causing the project of emancipation to fail. Angela Davis, who is among those to be credited for lending the term 'abolition' the popularity it has today, has thus insisted on the ongoing actuality of the project of abolition: the struggle against the manifold instances of state-inflicted violence (such as the military, prison, and police) stands in the tradition of that struggle for full emancipation; just as the abolition of slavery could not fully be accomplished without inventing new educational and democratic institutions, liberating people from carceral institutions also requires 'material resources that would enable them to fashion new, free lives'.[221]

The focus on the material side of political participation and on the creation of true accountability was an important corrective to the merely formal conception of democracy in bourgeois society, which proved all too compatible with economic exploitation and white supremacy. Abolition democracy, according to Angela Davis, thus corresponds to 'socialist rather than capitalist conceptions of democracy', demanding '**substantive** as well as formal rights, the right to be free of violence, the right to employment, housing, healthcare, and quality education'.[222] This emphasis on the importance on the *social* dimension, however, also tends to neglect the genuinely *political* aspect of the process of liberation. Liberation, in the democratic sense envisioned by Du Bois, means to gain collective agency to consciously shape the conditions of communal life. Democracy thus involves a notion of collective political autonomy, usually expressed in a particular set of institutions that are supposed to enable self-determination and self-government. Besides the material (or 'substantive') conditions for participation, this *does* also imply formal elements, such as a 'constitution' or charter defining the general scope and framework for collective rule-making, an arrangement for public deliberation, and procedural rules for decision-making.

To specify the genuinely *democratic* aspect of abolition democracy, a closer theoretical exchange between abolitionism and democratic theory might be fruitful. The collective creation of binding rules is not just a particular decision-making technique but has far-reaching **normative** implications. Historically speaking, the concept of law manifests the promise of freedom: it emancipates people from the brute force of nature as well as from **naturalized** forms of domination. In giving liberation the institutional form of the law, democracy not only disburdens individuals of the unbearable pressure of constantly having to make moral decisions in their everyday life by turning over the responsibility for decision-making to the collective, thus allowing individuals to temporarily withdraw from the social arena, it also creates specific interpersonal relationships based on norms of horizontal mutual respect. In including each other in a process of collective deliberation and decision-making, the members of a community express that they recognize each other as equal co-authors of binding norms, enabling the individual to develop a **subjectivity** based on self-affirmation and self-esteem. For this to be possible, however, for this 'binding' not to be posited in a heteronomous way, individual commitment has to be given under conditions where authentic and voluntary affirmation is possible. One consequence of this is that democracy cannot be limited to the moment of rule-making and then be suspended in the everyday rule-following – applying and interpreting the rules are also political issues open for democratic challenges.

As the abolitionist critique has shown, the establishment of coercive institutions such as the police thwarts the realization of these democratic ideals (the executive tends to become independent from the legislature; the police in their everyday interactions undermine the democratic standing of some of the citizens; and investment in carceral institutions weakens the social security needed to meaningfully participate in decision-making processes). The point of Benjamin's notion of a deposition of law was then to create the conditions for the authentic actualization of those ideals by liberating the law from the violence that had contaminated it. This presupposes that, contrary to a widely accepted doctrine, law is not *per se* coercive – rather, coercion is a historically specific *attribute* of law (namely a bourgeois, capitalist, state-enforced law). Benjamin's notion of a deposition of law enables us to reconcile the promises of democracy – even with its irreducible 'formalistic' aspects – with an abolitionist critique of oppression and exploitation by eliminating the violent remainders from the law.[223] We can thus conceptualize collective legislation without coercive execution, in other words: an abolition democracy.

To give this concept more plasticity, it is helpful to consider a point made by a democratic theorist who situates himself not at all in the abolitionist tradition: Jürgen Habermas. In line with Benjamin's praise of 'the conference, considered as a technique of civil agreement',[224] Habermas argued that language has a transformative effect on both subjectivity and sociality: collective deliberations can create the capacities required for social integration. This is because the condition for a rational discourse is the will of all participants to accept for themselves commitments that are relevant for post-discourse interactions. Habermas' point is now that a shared deliberation not only requires such a readiness, but also produces it: the discussion itself releases what he calls 'binding energies'.[225] We know this from everyday life: if we feel that our voice has actually been heard in a decision-making process, we are more willing to comply with the decision even if we were initially against it, simply because we value the decision-making process as such. Communicative action thus opens up the individual strategic perspective to the interests, needs, and desires of others and thereby initiates a learning process that in turn validates and stabilizes those radical-democratic institutions.

To be sure, contrary to what Habermas himself believed, this trust in collective decision-making can only evolve if the formal side of democracy is indeed accompanied by a material (or 'substantive') side (if people have not only the formal right but also the material possibility to participate, and if the decision actually affects the social, economic, political, and cultural foundations of communal life), and if the physical and psychological integrity of all is guaranteed (trust can only be generated in an atmosphere of safety and respect) – as abolitionist movements in their socialist and feminist manifestations have called for. But they also have to include procedural elements: it is only through collective deliberation and decision-making that language can replace violence as the major medium of social integration. If legislative acts could meaningfully reconfigure established social structures and if the deliberations that precede them were radically inclusive and participatory, violent execution through the police could be replaced through voluntary implementation of that which has been collectively decided.

Taken together, these elements – *deposing the law* and *abolishing state power* as a socialist, feminist, and radical-democratic project – offer an image of a society freed from state-inflicted violence. Unlike Benjamin, many abolitionist movements have understood abolition precisely *not* as a future event, initiating a 'new historical epoch' – but as an everyday practical activity of building alternative institutions. Following the anarchist idea of **prefigurative politics**, understood as an experimental construction of new communal relations within the old world, countless groups have practically empowered disenfranchised subjects through combining the establishment of a social infrastructure with creating conditions for accountability and healing, and horizontal and inclusive decision-making arrangements.[226] It is through the courageous and enduring experiments of those groups that someday we might find a more ambitious answer to Benjamin's question: 'whether there are no other than violent means for regulating conflicting human interests'.[227]

———

Daniel Loick teaches political and social philosophy at the University of Amsterdam. He works on critical theories of state-violence as well as subaltern forms of sociality. His book *A Critique of Sovereignty* came out in 2018 with Rowman & Littlefield.

POLICING AND COERCION
WHAT ARE THE ALTERNATIVES?

Guy Aitchison

———————

T
he 17th century **liberal** philosopher John Locke famously asked his readers to imagine a 'state of nature' in which individuals interact with one another without government or (human-made) law. This state of nature, he suggested, would operate according to a rough-and-ready system of DIY justice. If someone attacks me or steals my food, it is up to me to find and punish the transgressor. The problem with this situation, he suggests, is that no one can be trusted to act in a fair and impartial way when it comes to enforcing their own rights and the rights of those close to them. Self-love makes a person angry, passionate and over-zealous when he is 'judge in his own case'.[228] The state of nature, for Locke, is therefore characterised by uncertainty. Each of us is liable to the arbitrary judgment of our fellows and the quest for revenge easily spills over into tit-for-tat violence. The well-known solution that Locke and later liberals have proposed to this problem is a system of public rules, known to everyone in advance, and enforced against all by impartial

arbiters. According to this ideal of the 'rule of law', those who enforce the rules should themselves be constrained and accountable.

In contemporary societies, the enforcement function of states is discharged by centralised professional police forces procedurally authorised to use coercion. The problem, however, is that the existence of the police reproduces the danger of arbitrary power and violence in a different, more concentrated form. Each of us now confronts the power of a well-resourced, permanent body of trained public enforcers. Identifying with the interests of the state, the police often act to disrupt and suppress political challenges to the *status quo*.[229] Rather than being impartial, they may defer to the interests of those at the top of the social **hierarchy**, enforcing race and class-based oppression. In many cases, they are heavily armed and **militarised**.[230] When called to account for their abuses, police officers tend to close ranks and protect their own.[231]

There are of course far-reaching reforms of the police that can and should be carried out – restraining their legal powers, disarming them of offensive weaponry, tackling institutional racism and ensuring proper legal accountability for abuses. But should we do away with the institution of the police itself? And is it even possible? In this chapter, I sketch what alternatives to modern policing an emancipated society might employ from the standpoint of **normative analytical** political theory.[232] It is striking just how little has been written about the institution of the police within this field, aside from some mostly indirect discussion in ethical debates on racial profiling, immigration controls, surveillance and other related issues. While normative theorists have had a great deal to say about the abstract justification of coercive law, they have had considerably less to say about the main institution through which people experience that coercion in their everyday lives: the police. This is true even of 'realist' political theorists who call for a deeper engagement with real-world institutions and stress the methodological centrality of coercion and violence.[233] The unspoken implication of all this is the default conservative assumption that we cannot do without the police in something like their current form. In this chapter, I interrogate this assumption and reflect on the preconditions for a radically democratic society without present-day policing.

Any theoretical objection to the police should, I think, be formulated separately from an objection to the laws that the police currently enforce. There are many unjust laws (such as those covering non-violent drug offences) that the police currently enforce and many injustices (such as selling arms to dictators) that they entirely ignore. The obvious response to this fact is not to get rid of the police, but to make the laws more just. The concept of policing is also distinct from the concept of punishment, though the two are connected. A society could completely do away with the current system of prisons and punishment, choosing, for example, a system based purely on transformative justice (see chapters by Sarah Lamble and Melanie Brazzell in this collection). But it would not necessarily be inconsistent for this society to keep police officers to physically intervene while harms and violence are being committed or to identify those whose wrongful actions make them candidates for transformative accountability processes.

What is conceptually distinctive of the police, I suggest, is the *procedural authorisation to use coercion* – that is to say, the use of legally sanctioned threats and physical force, including powers of arrest and detention. There are of course many other non-coercive things that modern bureaucratic police forces do, such as gathering and analysing forensic evidence, intervening in cases of attempted suicide, victim liaison, and so on. But it is hard to imagine the police *as police* without the ultimate power to physically force people to obey the law – a power the state claims as **legitimate**. Two key features of the police as an institution, then, are that it is: i) a permanent standing body of professionally trained **agents** who are; ii) procedurally authorised to enforce the law through coercion.

As far as I know, there is no evidence of a society ever having existed without some kind of socially sanctioned coercion. Indeed, given everything we know about human beings, it is difficult to imagine even the most utopian society eliminating the need for *any* interventions to enforce moral rights and obligations. But this still leaves open the question of whether coercion is hierarchically organised and concentrated or more horizontal and dispersed. What is most disturbing from the standpoint of human freedom, I think, is the idea of a permanent standing bureaucracy of state agents with their own institutional self-interest and liable to use their power for oppressive purposes.

But is such a system unavoidable? Consider a more emancipated society that has managed to overcome many of the pathologies that arise from the current system of law enforcement. There are no anti-drug laws, for example, which criminalise whole swathes of the population and fuel gang-related violence. Drug addiction is treated as a public health issue, minimising the danger of interpersonal violence. Mental health is not treated as a matter for criminal law enforcement and prisons are either abolished or else radically re-envisaged in line with an emancipatory ideal of transformative justice. An idealised society of this kind would, I assume, still need rules to regulate and co-ordinate social interaction and promote desired behaviours. But let us assume that this is done through laws and/or social conventions that are themselves broadly just.

What alternatives might there be to the police in this society? There are, I think, two general strategies: those that *enhance compliance* with rules of desired behaviour and those that *challenge noncompliance*.

Enhancing compliance:

1) *Harmony of interests*: In an emancipated society, each person has their basic needs (to housing, food, health, education, and so on) taken care of and extensive opportunities for self-fulfilment. The benefits of social co-operation are shared.

2) *Mutual recognition*: There is a strong community ethos and people are disposed to mutually respectful relations. To the extent possible, hierarchies based on class, race, gender and other group identities have been overcome.

3) *Democratic equality*: Important political decisions are made through a system of strong inclusive democracy where each member of the community is heard on an equal basis. No one feels permanently estranged from this process.

4) *Benign social monitoring*: Strong social bonds are generated by communal living. People are familiar with their neighbours and others in their area and feel themselves accountable to them.

A great deal of progress towards a police-free world could, I think, be made through compliance-enhancing mechanisms 1 to 4. A situation of voluntary compliance is optimal since it avoids the more complicated question of enforcement and its associated costs for individuals and society at large. I suspect that under these social conditions we would see a great reduction in interpersonal harm and violence, but that the phenomenon itself would stubbornly persist.

In a society embodying (1), the social conditions behind a great deal of property offences will have been removed. Yet the existence of 'white collar crime' indicates that having enough isn't sufficient to prevent people wanting more through unlawful means. A far less competitive and individualistic culture would mitigate some of the worst of this behaviour, but it is unlikely to do away with all of it. Meanwhile, a society that has eliminated racism, sexism, homophobia, and other forms of social oppression, in accordance with (2), will have eliminated the **ideologies** that validate a considerable amount of interpersonal domination. Presumably, however, there would still be interpersonal coercion and violence motivated by anger, resentment and feelings of disrespect that are not rooted in **structural inequalities**. There are also a large number of dangerous behaviours – such as speeding – prompted by temporary personal advantage.

The thought behind (3) is that compliance is more likely where each person has the prospect of influencing the future direction of society on equal terms with others. It is not the simplistic view that people break the law only because they disagree with the rule they are breaking. Rather, thoroughgoing democratisation would lead people to feel less **alienated** from social institutions and less inclined to defect from the rules when it is in their short-term interests.[234] This in turn connects with (4) and the thought that an emancipated society would be one with strong community ties and networks. In such a society, it is possible to envisage a benign form of reciprocal social surveillance in operation. People would be less likely to unjustly harm others or put them at risk because they would feel themselves accountable to a wider community. Yet, while the addition of (3) and (4) may further reduce the need for socially sanctioned coercion, it is unlikely to eliminate it entirely. Even under the most optimistic assumptions, it seems naive to think that *all* rights violations and other forms of harm can be traced to social inequalities and alienation.

Through what methods, then, can any remaining noncompliance be addressed without reproducing the existing institution of the police? Consider these four possibilities, each of which involves coercion, but through more diffuse and informal methods:

A) *Victim justice*: Victims of injustice (and their friends) take responsibility for stopping and apprehending their transgressors.

B) *Bystander justice*: Those who observe an injustice taking place or become aware of such an injustice take responsibility for enforcing the rules against offenders.

C) *Delegated justice*: Where an injustice becomes known, the community collectively authorises a temporary body of individuals with responsibility for enforcing the rules against the offender.

D) *Rotating justice*: Members of the community take turns in enforcing the rules. A permanent body is authorised to use coercion, but one made up of community members who ordinarily have other social roles, in the manner of jury service.

Strategy (A) gives a central role to victims. Notably, there are examples of self-help justice even in today's society, which are often hailed as laudable forms of empowerment. Think of indebted occupiers fighting home evictions by banks or women using social media to confront their sexual harassers.

One can imagine a future scenario where people have prepared themselves for this responsibility for self-defence, and with a set of rules that constrain the appropriate force that they can use. But the worry of revenge-seeking remains. Locke was surely right to argue that at least some people will end up being biased towards themselves and that this generates uncertainty and the risk of escalation. Some of this objectionable self-love would be mitigated by the communal measures already discussed, but I doubt all of it would be.

There is also the obvious fact that many people – especially the young, elderly and infirm – simply do not have the capacity to intervene to stop others from engaging in interpersonal harm and violence. This concern also limits the potential reach of (B) – bystander justice – as a general mode of enforcement. There is a certain ethical appeal to a vision of society where people take responsibility for protecting one another and the fate of each person matters to all. But many of us would not be suited to this role and it is unclear how bystander-based justice would work for dangerous or difficult-to-solve cases. Although it may have a role to play, it is unlikely to be the only means of enforcement in an emancipated society.

Mechanisms (C) and (D) bring us closer to the concept of today's police in that they consist in bodies that are collectively regulated. A crucial difference, however, is that they do not involve a permanent standing body of officials, but something temporary. In a system of delegated justice

– (C) – the community convenes to appoint a sub-set of its members to act as enforcers. This body would be selected for its capabilities, expertise, and so on, and would operate according to a defined remit only so long as needed to deal with the specific offence under consideration. This would reduce the arbitrariness involved in (A) and (B) and would be more dependable, since it does not rely upon a victim or bystander happening to be present. A significant drawback, however, is that it is wholly reactive. It requires an injustice to have been committed and the citizen body to be convened before action is taken. Its potential for deterring and preventing harmful law-breaking is therefore limited.

What about (D), a rotating system of justice? Imagine a system where members of society are selected among those deemed capable to act as enforcers for a time-limited period of, say, one year. They could be elected, chosen at random via lottery or through some other method. One of the chief virtues of the existing jury system in criminal trials is that it functions as a check on the entrenched power of state interests. On many occasions, juries have shown leniency and refused to convict sympathetic defendants despite clear evidence of law-breaking.[235] Perhaps a rotating system of civic enforcers would have similar virtues. They could build the capacity and skills needed for their role, be subject to clear constraints, and accountable to the collective citizen body for how they discharge their role.

An advantage of this system is that those who perform the role of enforcer will not be permanent agents of the state. Unlike the police, they are unlikely to become an institutional lobby group for ever greater powers, weaponry and resources. They would, instead, be ordinary citizens with a certain degree of detachment from their role and lacking the disturbing group mentality and aggressive culture associated with a permanent standing institution. An obvious objection is that these enforcers would lack the effectiveness of a professional police force, raising the spectre of amateurishness. When a member of the public takes part in jury service, they are required to exercise skills of deliberation and judgment, which we presume all competent adults possess. The practice of policing – from the use of proportionate restraints, to compiling DNA evidence – is more tough and technical, requiring specialist skills. Perhaps this could be addressed by a process of collective capacity-building, or through longer terms of service for enforcers, but the worry is that the more the role becomes institutionalised, the more it starts to resemble the present-day police force.

Based on this brief sketch, is police abolition possible? Given everything we know about human societies to date, the idea of a community without *any* socially sanctioned coercion looks like a pipe dream. But great steps forward in reducing interpersonal harm and violence – and hence the need for social coercion – could be made through egalitarian and democratic reforms of the kind I have discussed. In such a society, bystander and victim-led justice would probably have a role to play, though their unreliable nature means that more coordinated and systematic approaches are likely to be needed. Here, there is an undeniable trade-off between professionalism, on the one hand, and the dangers of domination and oppression that come from having a permanent standing body of enforcers, on the other. It may be that an emancipated society simply chooses to accept a more rough-and-ready enforcement system, with some rule-breaking left unresolved, as a worthwhile price to pay for greater human freedom. Naturally, this kind of trade-off would be much more palatable in an emancipated society where the inequalities and alienation at the root of much interpersonal harm and violence have been overcome.

———————

Guy Aitchison is a political theorist with interests in human rights, political resistance and democratic theory. He is a lecturer in politics and international studies at Loughborough University and has been politically active in anti-austerity, migrant rights and democratic reform campaigns.

PRACTISING EVERYDAY ABOLITION

Sarah Lamble

Abolition is not absence, it is presence. What the world will become already exists in fragments and pieces, experiments and possibilities. So those who feel in their gut deep anxiety that abolition means knock it all down, scorch the earth and start something new, let that go. Abolition is building the future from the present, in all of the ways we can.

Ruth Wilson Gilmore[236]

Abolition can seem like a daunting task. We live in a world that is saturated with the assumption that police and prisons are necessary to address widespread problems of violence and harm. Even amongst those who recognise that police and prisons do not make us safe and instead perpetuate inequality, violence and harm, it can still feel hard to imagine life without these institutions.[237]

But as leading abolitionist thinker and organiser Ruth Wilson Gilmore reminds us, abolition is not simply about getting rid of the prisons, police or systems of surveillance and punishment; it is about what we build in their place. 'Abolition is about abolishing the conditions under which prison became the solution to problems, rather than abolishing the buildings we call prisons'.[238] Likewise, we cannot simply do away with the police – we need to address the conditions in which people feel that police are the only or best option for responding to harm in their lives. We must build other means for preventing and addressing harm that will actually keep us safe.

Part of that task means not treating abolition as a singular or revolutionary 'event' but as an ongoing process and practice. Abolition is a way of life and a collective approach to social change. It requires us to engage in strategies that dismantle the structures, institutions and systems that underpin and sustain prisons and police while at the same time building up systems of care, well-being, and support that fulfil human needs and enable communities to flourish. Abolition requires the double work of engaging in what abolitionists call 'non-reformist reforms'[239] – strategies that reduce the power and scope of the criminal justice system and reduce our reliance on it – while simultaneously building up our skills, capacity, and resources for alternative systems of preventing, addressing and responding to harm.[240]

Such change means practising *everyday abolition*. Everyday abolition is a means to connect efforts toward structural change with our everyday cultures and practices. Everyday abolition means undoing the cultural norms and mindsets that trap us within **punitive** habits and logics. There are many different ways of approaching this, but below are four key strategies.

1. Undo carceral cultures: identify and challenge punitive logics in everyday contexts.

The **carceral** is everywhere. Look around and we see punitive logics in our schools, our workplaces, our public services, our families, our relationships. The carceral is embedded in the social norms and institutions we inhabit. It is culturally engrained in our consciousness.

By 'carceral', abolitionists refer to logics and practices that normalise punitive responses to harm. It's the 'common sense' logic that equates justice with punishment. When a harm occurs, carceral logics encourage us to locate the cause of the problem in an individual (bad choices, inherent evil, poor upbringing, cultural deficiencies, monstrous **otherness**, etc.) and then isolate and punish that individual – and often stigmatise the community that person is part of. Sometimes this is done overtly – by the state and the criminal justice system or when someone calls the cops on someone else – but it's also done in more subtle everyday ways that normalise vindictive or punitive behaviour or celebrate redemptive violence. These punitive logics seep into our daily interactions at work, at school, at home, in our neighbourhoods and in our organising communities.

For example:

- A kid 'misbehaves' in class, so we exclude them from the classroom.

- Our lover says something hurtful, so we give them the cold shoulder.

- A work colleague does something we don't like, so we publicly shame them in front of other co-workers.

- A neighbour is dealing drugs from their flat, so we report them to the council even though they will likely get evicted and be made homeless as a result.

- An organisation that we are in coalition with uses language or strategies we think are oppressive, so we simply stop working with them.

- A prisoner who needs housing support upon release has a conviction for sexual violence, so no one will assist them.

- We humiliate or denigrate people on social media or encourage others to 'cancel' them when we don't like what they say.

- We get our daily moral workout by consuming media that encourages us to divide the world into good and bad, those deserving of empathy and those we demonise and abandon.

While most of these examples are not direct forms of state policing and violence, they all can contribute to carceral cultures that normalise punishment and isolation as a response to social problems. Instead of addressing a problem directly or figuring out why the problem has arisen, we are encouraged to react with blame, retaliation and punishment. We try to address the problem by removing the person from our community, marking them out as fundamentally different from the rest of 'us' and by distancing ourselves from them. These patterns often play out along class, racial and disability lines. For example, the kids who are most likely to be removed from school are those who are **racialised**, from disadvantaged backgrounds or have learning disabilities.[241] Instead of asking why the education system isn't meeting their needs or what else is going on for them, we label the kid as the 'problem' and try to remove them.

A key task for everyday abolition is to identify and challenge carceral logics that creep into our daily practices. This isn't always easy. The line between setting **legitimate** boundaries versus punishing and isolating others is not always straightforward. More importantly, none of us are immune to the wider cultural norms that constantly equate justice with punishment. These narratives are deeply engrained and internalised and it takes work to identify and unravel them – particularly if we feel emotionally invested in punitive or retaliatory responses. Punishment can feel seductively good in the moment, but rarely generates the resolution, healing or long-term change we are ultimately seeking.

Abolitionists argue that if we don't challenge these carceral logics and practices at the everyday level, it's hard to challenge them at institutional levels. It's easy to be an abolitionist in theory. Putting it into practice requires ongoing effort and reflection. That's why everyday abolition needs to be a collective effort to push back against the individualisation of social problems. We need to support each other to figure out how to do things differently, to build the world we want.

This does not mean that we shouldn't challenge harmful behaviours or hold people accountable. It means that we need to respond with strategies that are not about escalating harm through individual punishment. To do this, we need a second strategy in our everyday abolition toolkit: a support-based rather than punishment-based framework for responding to harm.

2. Shift our everyday responses to harm: we need to stop responding to harm with punishment and isolation and instead offer support, safety, healing and connection – even when it's hard.

When someone hurts another person, there are two common tendencies: one is to deny or minimise that harm (say it didn't happen, or it doesn't matter, or it wasn't as bad as it seems); the other is to blame, demonise and retaliate (the harm-doer is terrible and should be punished or separated from the community).[242] The first tendency is common when we care about or love the person that did the harm; the second tendency is common when we love or are close to the person who experienced the harm. But neither of these strategies are effective because they don't actually address the impact of the harm. The responses also don't address why harm occurred in the first place or what can be done to prevent it from happening in the future.

Offering support, safety and healing is important for *both* the person or people that experienced the harm *and* the person or people who did the harm. That support needs to be focussed on the specific and immediate needs of the situation and the people affected, whilst also considering how to address the wider conditions that led to the harm. It is also important to recognise that harm is a collective problem (with collective consequences) and therefore requires collective solutions. Harm enacted by an individual rarely occurs in complete isolation. The behaviour and conditions that led to the harm are often normalised, condoned, ignored, enabled or even supported by others. This is particularly the case for interpersonal violence, including childhood sexual abuse.[243]

Instead of responding to harm with punishment, we need to build infrastructures of support and care – culturally, institutionally and in our daily lives. This is often easier in theory than in practice, particularly when a harm occurs to someone we love or is enacted by someone we dislike; it can be easy to fall into punitive logics and practices. But even when harm is done by people we disapprove of or people who repeatedly act in harmful ways, we need to ask why those harms are occurring and address the needs of everyone involved. We need to look at the broader context and not just at the individual.

Carceral logics teach us that there are good people and bad people, victims and perpetrators, innocent and guilty. We are taught to respond to people as one or the other. But reality is much more complex. Many people who harm others have also been harmed. Experiencing harm doesn't prevent you from harming others. Just look at the demographics of who is locked up in prison and it is clear that the most socially disadvantaged and discriminated against populations end up there. That doesn't mean that people in prison haven't engaged in harmful behaviour or that we need to resort to claims of 'innocence' in order to challenge the injustices of imprisonment. Rather, we need to be able to hold the reality that people can be *both* harm-doer and harmed; we need to recognise that people can do terrible things but still need support and care. We need to embrace a politics of 'no one is disposable'.[244]

Part of our task is to better understand and interrupt patterns where hurt generates further hurt. For example, people sometimes respond to trauma by lashing out and hurting others. Or people exert power over and abuse others in relation to their own feelings of powerlessness or vulnerability. This does not in any way excuse or condone abusive acts, but it means that if we want to challenge that behaviour, increasing a harm-doer's vulnerability through isolation, shaming or punishment is unlikely to work. Responding to one form of violence by enacting another form of violence is not only ineffective, it is counterproductive and exacerbates cycles of harm.

Shifting our responses away from punishment is particularly difficult when it comes to sexual violence; people who are committed to abolitionist principles sometimes make exceptions when it comes to sexual violence and gendered harm. There can be an assumption that people who commit sexual violence are somehow different or irredeemable. But as feminist abolitionists have long argued, sexual and gender violence is so widespread and pervasive that it needs to be at the centre of our abolitionist responses. 'Sexual exceptionalism' will not enable us to meaningfully address it. The reality is that most sexual violence is not committed by strangers, but by people we know and often love. This is partly why it can be so difficult to address.[245]

Advocates for transformative justice[246] argue that instead of responding to harm with punishment, we must enact forms of 'love-centred accountability' or 'compassionate accountability'.[247] This means finding ways to support each other when we or others have done harmful things. It means focussing on reducing harm and preventing it from happening again.[248] To do this, we need a third strategy, which is about capacity building.

3. Build our collective skills and capacity to prevent harm and to foster everyday accountability and reparation.

Responding to harm with support and care requires us to build up our collective skills and capacities. If we can train people in first aid and emergency CPR, we can also teach safe bystander inventions, violence de-escalation, conflict resolution and harm reduction. We can learn the early signs of abusive relationships and support each other to intervene before things escalate. We can find ways to support each other to heal from our own and collective traumas.

Part of this work involves identifying the many ways we already can and do respond to harm without resorting to policing, punishment and retaliation. When a problem comes up, we can consider the different ways we could potentially address it without relying on police or prisons (and without becoming police-like or punitive ourselves).

As the Creative Interventions Project recognises,[249] people's immediate community (whether it be family, friends, neighbours, co-workers and even acquaintances) are often much better placed to intervene in, and respond to, everyday harm than the formal criminal justice system. So we all need to skill up to feel able and confident to intervene. We shouldn't assume that only professionals can act to address violence. Groups like Hollaback, for example, are teaching people ways of intervening in everyday sexual harassment through safe bystander interventions.[250]

We also need to think about accountability as a daily practice and skill we all need to foster, rather than something that is exceptional or delegated to others. As Ann Russo, author of the book *Feminist Accountability*,[251] describes:

> If taking accountability for harm became a daily practice, rather than solely something that we demand of others in egregious situations, then taking accountability would be less fraught with guilt, shame, defensiveness, punishment, and retaliation. It would create more compassion for one another when we make mistakes, when we speak and act in harmful and oppressive ways (intentionally or unintentionally),

and/or contribute to harm in some way. And it would make it easier to admit wrongdoing.[252]

Part of this shift means actively recognising that we ourselves may be the harm-doers or harm-enablers. Too often we are invested in aligning ourselves with the good and the innocent, and in distancing ourselves from the guilty and the harm-doers. Everyday abolition requires us to acknowledge we are all capable of harm just as we are all vulnerable to being harmed. This doesn't mean that the distribution of harm is equal; we know that harm and violence is deeply connected to structures of power that render some bodies more vulnerable than others. But we must understand our role in enabling or upholding structures of power that produce violence and impact on the distribution of life chances.

Confronting our complicity with violence can be painful, but it is crucial for ending harm, particularly when it comes to violence within our homes, families and social institutions. One of the most painful aspects of coming to terms with the pervasiveness of childhood sexual abuse, for example, can be acknowledging the extent to which other people knew about it and didn't act. Or that people didn't listen or believe survivors when they made brave disclosures.[253] Sometimes we refuse to see or believe what is right in front of us. We can often fail to recognise our own harmful behaviour and resist being accountable. As Russo notes:

> There are few spaces to talk about the harms we've caused and the systems of oppression in which we've been complicit. Mostly it seems that when confronted,

we try to prove that we are not responsible – to prove our 'innocence'. Or we try to blame others, or to claim that we are the real victims.[254]

We can all make accountability part of our everyday abolition practice. As Kai Cheng Thom writes:

> When we are able to admit that the capacity to harm lies within ourselves – within us all – we become capable of radically transforming the conversation around abuse and rape culture. We can go from simply reacting to abuse and punishing 'abusers' to preventing abuse and healing our communities. Because the revolution starts at home, as they say. The revolution starts in your house, in your own relationships, in your bedroom. The revolution starts in your heart.[255]

There are many grassroots organisations doing important work to challenge everyday carceral logics and to build collective capacity for support, healing and accountability. Many of these projects have developed simple tools and resources that can help us extend the skills we already have and channel them into everyday harm reduction and violence prevention work.[256]

We already have many of the tools and resources we need to stop violence – particularly amongst communities where calling the cops was never an option because of the threat of violence or deportation, where alternatives have been necessary for survival.[257] But we also need to develop new tools and resources, particularly for survivors of violence. As Darnelle L. Moore notes in *Love with Accountability: Digging*

Up the Roots of Childhood Sexual Abuse, 'the tools that many people need to heal have yet to be imagined and created'.[258]

This work takes ongoing practice. It is not something we can attend one training session on or read one article about and then know how to respond to or address every situation. As transformative justice advocate and anti-violence organiser Ejeris Dixon puts it, 'We must practice community safety as we would practice an instrument or a sport. By practicing in slow, measurable, and deliberate ways, we build the knowledge we need to diffuse and address conflict within our communities.'[259]

4. Connect the everyday to the big picture.

Finally, none of these everyday practices will be enough unless we connect them to larger, long-term goals. As the LGBTQ+ anti-violence group Community United Against Violence reminds us, violence exists internally (within ourselves), interpersonally (between people) and institutionally (between institutions and individuals).[260] Work to address violence needs to happen at all three levels. We need to link the micro and the macro so that our everyday efforts are contributing to the broader social, systemic and institutional change that will make a world without prisons and police become possible.

This means we need to consider how the tactics we implement today will impact on the medium- and longer-term strategies for the future. We don't want to enact strategies today that we'll have to undo at a later point. We need to dismantle and transform the institutions and structures that normalise prisons, police and punishment. This means supporting campaigns to stop prison expansion, redirect police budgets and reduce the size of criminal punishment systems. It also means organising for housing, health care, racial and economic justice, climate emergency and clean water campaigns, disability justice, labour rights, reproductive justice, decolonial struggles and broader social justice campaigns – these are all part of abolitionist work.

While abolition can sometimes feel daunting, it is important to keep in mind that much collective work and effort is already being done to make possible abolitionist futures. Connecting to, and building on, that existing work is essential for producing sustainable and collective social change. We need to do the work of lifting up and joining together various struggles that comprise the many different facets of abolitionist work. We can take hope and inspiration in the creativity, collectivity and determination that is found in both the daily efforts and the wider struggles for abolition that occur across the globe. These connected abolitionist efforts are what enable us to do the work in the here and now that gets us closer to the world we want in the future.

———

Sarah Lamble is a founding member of the Bent Bars Project, which coordinates a letter-writing programme for LGBTQ+ prisoners in Britain. Lamble also organises with Abolitionist Futures and teaches at Birkbeck, University of London, researching issues of sexuality, imprisonment and transformative justice.

THEORIZING TRANSFORMATIVE JUSTICE

COMPARING CARCERAL AND ABOLITIONIST SELVES, AGENCIES, AND RESPONSIBILITIES

Melanie Brazzell

S eeing Harvey Weinstein sentenced for sexual assault was a bittersweet, confusing moment. The abolitionist in me knows that prison, even for the elite who rarely see the inside of a cell, is never going to solve rape culture. If interpersonal violence is rooted in the broader social structures of violence that organize our society, then removing 'bad apples' cannot heal a rotting tree. As lawyer and activist Dean Spade has said, the prison *itself* is the serial rapist and the serial murderer.[261] But the survivor in me was moved to see sexual violence publicly recognized and wealthy, white men's impunity punctured by the ferociousness of the #MeToo movement.

These feelings of being caught in a cross-current are not an accident – they've been socio-historically engineered by systems that have told survivors for years that the criminal legal system is synonymous with justice. INCITE!, a network of US-based feminists of color, point out the limits of this engineering in order to reframe the debate: 'The question is not, should she call the police. The questions are, why is that her only option, and can we provide other options that will keep her truly safe.'[262]

GENDER-BASED VIOLENCE AS ALIBI & OUTCOME

Gender-based violence appears as somewhat of a puzzle when we talk about abolition.

On the one hand, sexual violence has been used as an alibi for the build-up of the **carceral** state in the US (and elsewhere) since the 1970s. The '**punitive** turn' around this time, when the government shifted its spending to repressive rather than preventive responses to social problems like poverty, homelessness, and drug addiction, used the specter of 'rapists' and 'sexual predators' to justify locking up ever greater numbers of people – disproportionately Black and Latinx. Some feminists saw opportunities to fund their rape crisis centers or advance their anti-sex work advocacy by joining forces with conservative, racist law-and-order politics, forging what scholars and activists have called 'carceral feminism'.[263] The carceral state has claimed to 'protect' women, but historical scholarship shows how the gender **binary** was created within **racial capitalism**, so that 'womanhood' itself was a status of sexual vulnerability and earned protection only permitted to white women, leaving Black and indigenous women legally 'unrapeable'.

On the other hand, sexual violence has not been solved by increased criminalization and harsher punishment. Few cases ever go to trial, and even those rarely bring what most survivors say they want: community recognition, healing and safety, and/or remorse, accountability, and change on the part of the perpetrator(s). In fact, women and queer of color activists and scholars have shown how the carceral state not only fails to keep its hollow promise to protect women and queer people, but actively harms them under the cover of this promise.[264] Sexual misconduct is the second most common form of police misconduct in the US, and the limited evidence indicates higher rates of domestic violence among police officers than in the general population.[265] Trans, indigenous, sex worker, undocumented, Black, queer, and many other marginalized survivors are often criminalized for their survival activities, self-expression, migration status, or self-defense (see, for instance, the work of Survived and Punished). Numerically, men have more contact with police and prisons, but the carceral state also extends to some of the 'feminized' sectors of the social welfare state, with which marginalized genders often have more contact. Social welfare, child protective services, and schools all include methods to surveil, discipline, criminalize, and punish women and queer people.

So gender-based violence appears as both an alibi for the carceral state and, at the same time, its outcome. It is mobilized as the most common argument against abolishing police and prisons ('well, what about the rapists?'), yet at the same time anti-violence activists have been on the front lines of abolition, pointing out the carceral state's failures. As founders of the transformative justice and community accountability movement, these women, queer, non-binary, and trans people of color have given us some of the most visionary alternatives to the police, particularly for sexual and partner violence.

WHAT IS TRANSFORMATIVE JUSTICE?

Multiply marginalized, queer people and women of color stand at the dangerous intersections of both state and interpersonal violence, and as such, are well positioned to recognize that one form of violence (like police) cannot be used to solve another (like rape and abuse). Yet Kimberlé Crenshaw argues that most social movements have made '**intersectional** failures' by not examining issues through the lens of women of color's experiences.[266] Transformative justice activists, at the crossroads of both anti-racist and feminist movements, have pointed out the need for both to recognize the contribution of the other:[267] interpersonal violence must be understood in the context of state violence and vice versa in order to develop responses that adequately respond to both race- and gender-based oppressions, and address the intersectional needs of survivors. The Black Lives Matter movement, led primarily by Black women and queer people, has shown what the integration of abolition and feminism can look like.

Over the past twenty years, these organizers, healers, artists, and teachers have experimented with holistic, community-based responses to sexual and relationship violence. These seek to address both concrete cases of harm as well as the underlying conditions that allowed the violence to happen, such that the harm cannot happen again. Out of this has grown a body of theory and practice organized under the umbrella terms *community accountability* & *transformative justice*.[268] These transformative justice (TJ) practitioners began primarily with cases of sexual and partner violence in their own activist groups, community organizations, neighborhoods, and families, and have expanded their focus to interpersonal violence and conflict more broadly (see groups like Project NIA and Creative Interventions).

INCITE!, the US network of feminists of color who coined the term 'community accountability' (CA), understands it to integrate four areas of work: survivor support and self-determination; perpetrator accountability and change; transforming community values and practices; and challenging the **structural conditions** that enable gender-based violence.[269] Rather than following a fixed, centralized model, most TJ-CA practices are experimental and contextual, varying in their focus on one or the other of these four areas. Some practitioners focus on survivor support and harm reduction, like sex workers developing their own community reporting, evidence collection, and surveillance systems to prevent assault by johns or police.[270] Others engage with those causing harm: groups like Philly Stands Up and Creative Interventions have developed models to facilitate accountability, rather than denial and shame, for people who've committed sexual assault. Still others explore how communities have stepped up to support both safety and accountability: de-escalated violence at parties and demonstrations (Safe OUTside the System Collective); used story-telling to open conversations about harm and healing (Story Telling and Organizing Project); and built networks of non-state resources for people to activate when facing mental health crises (Trans Lifeline, Oakland Power Projects, Icarus Project). This is the granular work of change, not a universal one-size-fits-all approach.

While this year marks the 20th anniversary of the founding of key TJ organizations, the movement is rooted in a much longer history of improvised, kitchen-table responses to violence, by women and queer people in Black, Brown, and indigenous communities where calling the police was not an option. This could mean opening your home to someone whose partner is acting violently, sending over respected elders to talk with that partner, or starting honest, painful conversations about violence in your mosque or church, at school, or in your own family. In searching for alternatives to the carceral state, TJ activists also drew upon indigenous justice traditions, since appropriated and popularized outside those communities as restorative justice. While restorative justice holds promise for change within institutions like schools, it has also often been co-opted as a supplemental arm of the criminal legal system.

In contrast, TJ responses stand outside of state institutions, rooted instead in social movements.

NEW JUSTICE MODEL: FROM CARCERAL LOGIC TO SOCIAL CONNECTION

I am particularly interested in how TJ practitioners are imagining new ways of relating to one another and new theories of justice, accountability, and safety. In my work, I argue that the movement makes four major shifts from existing concepts of justice towards transformative justice in the four areas that INCITE! identifies as central:

- in the realm of *structural conditions*, a shift from the **discourse** of individual moral liability to an accountability that links individual and structural responsibilities;

- in the sphere of *perpetrators*, a shift from punishment to accountability;

- in the realm of *survivors*, a shift from security as **paternalist** protection to safety as survivor self-determination;

- and lastly, in the sphere of the *community*, a shift from the state to the community as the relevant body for addressing interpersonal harm and creating justice.

These shifts are connected to a more general turn away from a carceral logic (discussed in Sarah Lamble's piece in this book) that seeks to individualize and isolate social problems and towards a politics of social connection as a potential solution. The crisis of sexual violence – and the violation of boundaries and injury to the self that it involves – becomes an impetus for the counterintuitive: for opening towards interdependency at the precise moment when social relations have wounded, and for seeing social connection as a resource at the moment when it appears most hazardous or precarious.

I want to explore one fragment of the theory of transformative justice I'm working on: comparing how carceral feminism and transformative justice understand the **subject**, **agency**, and responsibility, and thus what they believe the right response to violence should be.

CARCERAL VS ABOLITIONIST SELVES

The carceral self is atomistic, a cell alone against a hostile world that impinges upon him, facing a set of options (in theory, freely available to all) and choosing rationally based on self-interest. I say 'him' intentionally, because this model of a **sovereign** or self-governing subject originates in 17th century Europe in the Enlightenment philosophy of Immanuel Kant, in response to the rise of capitalism and a secular, modern world. In this world, only property-owning, European/white **cis-**men were seen as rational and thus sovereign. These men justified their oppression of marginalized groups by portraying them as unable to govern themselves, comparing them to children or animals. Over many generations of struggle, new subjects (Black, indigenous, migrant, trans, non-binary, women, disabled, **mad**) have fought to be recognized as worthy of self-determination and agency.

But why fight for a white man's concept of sovereignty? Rooted in their communities' experiences of resistance, some of those subjects held a radically different concept of who we are. This forms the basis of what I argue is a transformative justice model of the self: socially constructed both within relationships of intimacy, recognition, and care *and* through relationships of power, violence, and oppression. We are shaped by different levels of **intersubjectivity**, ranging from family to community to institutions to social structures, that traverse time (the intergenerational imprint of ancestors) and space (the experience of migration and **diaspora**).

The carceral is also an imagination, a way of seeing, that trains us to see objects and people as discrete and bordered units, ignoring the webs of relationship between them. The individual swims to the surface and the structural remains murky or invisible. Transformative justice invites us to view ourselves in new dimensions, where the individual and the structural both come into view together as co-constitutive, the way we might see an optical illusion or a 'Magic Eye' autostereogram. From the carceral point of view, violence originates in individual moral failure or pathology – the inability to 'govern myself' properly as a sovereign over the kingdom of the self. For transformative justice, harm and violence are a kind of contagious language, socially learned and reinforced – a behavior, not an identity, which can change with time and effort.

CARCERAL VS ABOLITIONIST AGENCY

What flows from the carceral subject is a model of responsibility that founds our criminal legal system, which philosopher Iris Marion Young calls 'the liability model'.[271] In it, you are responsible for actions you intentionally, knowingly, and voluntarily cause. Responsibility can only be attributed to actors with agency, able to exercise their self-determination by freely choosing their actions. When I talk with survivors about transformative justice, particularly those who are privileged, I witness the inner struggle to let go of a carceral imagination. If we accept that structures of violence shape and enable interpersonal acts of harm, does that let a perpetrator of sexual harm off the hook, for example if they themselves experienced abuse as a child or are exposed to the trauma of racism on a daily basis? Do they have less agency and, therefore, responsibility for their actions?

Some argue that oppression does indeed leave oppressed subjects with a failed agency, while others see this as a paternalistic excuse that disrespects a person's **autonomy**. What both sides share, however, is the assumption that **structural injustice** can only be seen as an extenuating circumstance, an impingement that might limit the sovereign, carceral subject's agency. The implicit norm is an unhindered, able-bodied freedom. Responsibility becomes an either/or: either you're fully responsible or you're not at all, with no in-between.[272] In the case of sexual violence, such an either/or can lead to either demonizing the person causing harm or minimizing and excusing their behavior,[273] with no room for the three-dimensionality and complexity of violence.

Carceral feminism appears as a kind of funhouse mirror of the fantasy of the sovereign subject. Violence's impact on agency isn't relevant only to perpetrators – in a carceral feminist framework, being a victim of sexual violence is also seen as something that permanently diminishes one's agency, justifying the idea that others must act on your behalf. I use the word 'victim' rather than 'survivor' here on purpose, since mainstream anti-violence advocacy has too often portrayed and treated people who experience harm as agency-less objects of pity, shock, and tragedy. Political theorist Wendy Brown has argued that many oppressed subjects become dangerously attached to their own woundedness, emphasizing injury and suffering to gain political recognition while losing sight of their own potential liberation.[274]

Alisa Bierria, philosopher and CA activist, uses Black feminist approaches to question the implicit norms of autonomy and efficacy attributed to privileged subjects, against which oppressed subjects' agency is measured.

'Instead of a binary or scaled model of agency that gauges subjects as having more or less, abled or disabled, or successful or failed agency, I propose a **heterogeneous** framework of agency—agencies'.[275] The implicit norm of agency as something possessed and exercised by subjects who are backed up by institutional power is marked by Bierria as merely one kind of agency among others, which she terms ***hegemonic*** *agency*. In contrast, there are agencies that seek to collectively undermine oppression, for which she coins the term *transformative agency*. Bierria invokes the image of a map, rather than a set of measurements, to assess heterogeneous agencies.

Beirria shares the story of Janice Wells, a Black woman who called the Georgia police out of fear that someone was prowling around her house. When white police officers arrived, they assumed without evidence that she was the victim of domestic violence, drawing on racist stereotypes about Black families. They questioned Wells about who was in her home, and she chose to refuse to answer. This attempt at protecting herself from police harm was misinterpreted by the officers as a refusal to cooperate, reframing her as a perpetrator. The police then tased and arrested her. According to Bierria, oppressed agents like Black women exercise agency but their actions are 'defined away from them'[276] by dominant perceptions of Blackness as inherently criminal, making their agency illegible in dominant frameworks of meaning. They are nevertheless 'authors' of their intentions, even if not socially 'authorized'.[277]

A transformative justice framework of abolitionist selves with heterogenous agencies affirms that our agency is not only limited by social structures but also enabled by them. The structurally privileged are therefore not less shaped by systems of power than those who are structurally oppressed, but simply differently shaped. Thus, acknowledging cycles of violence that lead perpetrators to cause harm serves as an explanation, not an excuse, in an abolitionist framework – it doesn't diminish agency or responsibility when we radically reconceive both. This new understanding of agency is relevant not only for how we see those who cause harm, but also for how we support those who experience it. It calls upon us to use our collective resources to support survivor power and action, to help their authorship become more legible, if not authorized.

CARCERAL VS ABOLITIONIST RESPONSIBILITY

Built on a carceral view of the self, which tends to deny the social relationships that form and sustain us, the liability model can only distribute responsibility to individuals. This responsibility works like a debt incurred by treading on the rights of others. I repay the debt through 'an eye for an eye' **retribution**, by being deprived of my rights in proportion to my wrongdoing. Accountability here means *taking account*: a mathematical calculation where violence is extracted out of its relational context in order to make equivalencies between different kinds of harms. Punishment is similarly made universal and measurable in the form of money (fines) or time (incarceration). This moral calculation distributes moral guilt and divides up the ownership of misdeeds in a moral economy that is binary and **affectively** loaded: those who cause harm are bad and blameworthy, while victims are innocent and morally intact.

In a transformative justice model, responsibility for causing harm is a non-retributive mode of response to my relations with others, relations which constitute me and which I cannot fully master or control. In a community accountability framework, harm is framed not primarily as a violation of rights but of specific human relationships. This calls for a community- and context-specific response, rather than the application of universal laws to a particular case, in order to repair and transform those relationships. Responsibility means *giving* (rather than taking) *account*. This story – or explanation, apology, eulogy – accepts responsibility for my choices and their consequences for those I have harmed, who are my audience. It allows me to critically examine the web of relations and structures that underpin my story and constitute me, and to *restory* myself with new lines of agency to make new choices without violence.[278] This is not a story of starting over clean and new, isolated from past selves and mistakes, but of building muscle to make better choices and shift habits over time. These changes happen in and through relationships, rather than through a sovereign self that remakes itself as infallible and secured against all future mistakes.

Community accountability involves many acts of giving account. Just as agency can be understood as heterogenous, so too can responsibility. TJ practitioners call for responsibility at multiple levels: by the one(s) who caused the harm, as well as those in the immediate community who facilitated or ignored the violence, as well as people who benefit from – and institutions that uphold – the structures that enabled the violence.

CONCLUSION

Carceral feminism's 'wounded attachments'[279] have led the mainstream anti-violence movement to uncritically appeal to the state and other powerful, **patriarchal** actors to take responsibility for ending sexual violence, rather than empowering survivors as liberation agents and movement makers. This vision of responsibility for violence is one of security, relying on a supposedly 'benevolent' masculine protection. Yet abolitionist feminist **critique** has demonstrated that the state's functions as protector and punisher are inseparable. State protection for survivors almost always involves repressive punishment, sometimes even for survivors themselves who face criminalization for their citizenship status, sex work, Blackness, queerness, or indigeneity. Hence, the 'violence of anti-violence'[280] when done through a lens of carceral selves, agency, and responsibility. I offer transformative justice's alternative visions of these categories as a critique and pathway out of this contradiction, this cross-current in which some survivors remain trapped.

'Both state and individual sovereignty require fixed boundaries, clearly identifiable interests and identities, and power conceived as generated and directed from within the entity itself'.[281] Playing with the term 'sovereignty' allows us to explore connections between carceral selves and carceral states. Just as transformative justice allows us to question the fantasy of individual sovereignty and autonomy, so too does it question state autonomy and sovereignty – giving us a lens that functions like an optical illusion to blur borders, question fixed identities, and recirculate power.

Transformative justice's vision of the self, agency, and responsibility are all embedded in webs of relationship, so it is no surprise that many TJ-CA practitioners point to community (not the courtroom) as the best setting for justice, healing, and prevention of harm. As many failed TJ experiments have taught us, we can't romanticize community or assume it already exists; sexual harm can leave a community in tatters or reveal to people that they are connected in ways they had previously denied. Members of the Northwest Network of Bi, Trans, Lesbian & Gay Survivors of Abuse have emphasized 'accountable communities' rather than 'community accountability' as the first step.[282] This means building healthy, honest relationships and a sense of community with shared values, and practicing holding ourselves and one another accountable in everyday, low-level circumstances (see Sarah Lamble's piece for more suggestions). This leaves us better prepared to respond when major acts of violence happen, relying on our own self-organized networks rather than the state. These alternatives needn't supplement but can also openly contest the state and its claims to sovereignty, including its right to define what justice can mean for survivors.

Melanie Brazzell is a transformative justice researcher and practitioner, and founder of the What *Really* Makes Us Safe? project. They are completing their dissertation at University of California Santa Barbara, and in response to wildcat strikes there, created Strike University. They use participatory research as a tool for social movements with the Momentum Community Research Council and the Realizing Democracy project.

BEYOND POLICING, FOR A POLITICS OF BREATHING

Vanessa E. Thompson

In a global moment defined by the spread of a novel coronavirus that puts large parts of the world on hold and in confinement, slows down time for some but not for others, we (again) see protests against policing igniting the streets worldwide – in the US, in Europe and in many parts in the **Global South** such as Kenya and Nigeria, India and Argentina. The killings of Breonna Taylor, George Floyd, Ahmaud Arbery, Tony McDade, Dion Johnson and many others in the US iteratively and brutally lay bare what it means to live, for centuries, at the receiving end of policing. The way the protests have travelled from various US-American cities to other parts of the world further shows that this condition is not confined only to the US. Quite the contrary, protesters and vulnerable communities are standing in solidarity with black people in the US as well as emphasising that policing unfolds as a violent and murderous condition in their various, respective contexts too. Names of black people who lost their lives at the hands of police in the US are called out and remembered in concert with names of black people who lost their lives at the hands of police in other parts of the African **diaspora**.

The protests also reveal that the ways the pandemic is being policed are just further functions of the **intersectional** injustices – those that unfold from interlocking systems of oppression, exploitation and violence (such as racism, **hetero-patriarchy**, class exploitation, colourism, **ableism**) – and the organisation of violence and abandonment produced by **racial gendered capitalism**.[283] Not only do we currently see a further expansion of policing, which raises the question why a global health crisis is met with further control and punishment instead of solidarity and extensions of care, but **racialised** and intersectionally vulnerable groups experience further brutalisation by police and related regimes of punishment and incarceration. This includes stop and frisk identity checks and pat downs even when social distancing has become a political norm in most countries (especially in the Global North).

On Friday April 10, 2020, Armen Henderson, a black internal medicine physician, was profiled and handcuffed by Miami police as he loaded his car with supplies that he wanted to bring to houseless people in downtown Miami.[284] He and his team at the University of Miami Health System were doing this weekly to support houseless people with much needed supplies such as tents, toiletries, and masks. He was on his way to support people who are especially vulnerable to the virus.

A further 'case'[285] that speaks to the experiences of being policed on an everyday basis, and the justified fear many black people and people of colour have of wearing homemade or even surgical masks, is the example of two black men who, early on in the pandemic, wore surgical masks and were profiled and followed by a police officer in a grocery store.[286] What is generally considered an act of solidarity in times of pandemic (wearing a mask) risks further criminalising racialised **subjects** and groups.

In the midst of the pandemic in France, various collectives and groups that are active in the underprivileged outskirts of French cities have released several videos of police violence against racialised and working class folks from the so-called *banlieues* – they are urging people to document and film these acts and calling for an immediate end to police violence in these racialised working class districts.[287] In Adana, Turkey, Ali El Hamdan, a Syrian teenager, was shot by police officers while on his way to work under the current restrictions on movement. Various self-organised sex workers' collectives have called and are organising for an end to further and intensified policing during the pandemic, which renders racialised and migrant sex workers even more vulnerable.[288]

There are many other 'examples' and though these contexts differ with regard to their histories, regimes of punishment, legal regulations and so on, we can observe a striking relation between policing, race, and further intersectional dimensions of oppression and dehumanisation (such as migration status, socio-economic exploitation, mental health, and gender) at work in all of them. That this relation becomes even more apparent – viral, even – in times of crisis, when vulnerable groups are actually in need of more support and solidarity rather than more policing and punishment, urges us to think more deeply about this relation. Nevertheless, it is far from limited to times of pandemic, as Derecka Purnell explains: 'We are at risk of police violence generally, and now specifically through this pandemic'.[289] Being at risk of police violence *generally*, as a lived experience and condition, stands in stark contrast to an understanding of policing as providing security and safety. This point of view also challenges **critiques** of policing that focus too exclusively on spectacular moments of excessive police violence such as at demonstrations. Experiences of everyday policing, which often go unnoticed and unseen by large parts of society (such as racial profiling in the form of stops, harassment and controls but also related forms of police violence that unfold along intersectional dimensions of power) thus provide a window for an **analysis** and critique of policing that begins from the perspectives of those for whom policing means risk and violence, even death, rather than safety, security and justice.

CONTINUITIES

It is helpful here to also look at the historical implications of being at risk of police violence *generally*, and how conjunctures of racism, colonial capitalism and (hetero-)patriarchy play into this. In the contexts of North America, black, and black feminist abolitionists especially, have delineated the connections between evolving practices of policing and the logics of black bondage and enslavement.[290] In his famous work *The Wretched of the Earth* Frantz Fanon looks at the role of policing in the colonies and explains that the dividing line between colonised groups and colonising formations of power is demonstrated by the police and the solider as 'the official, instituted go-betweens'[291] whose immediate presence and frequent and direct action towards colonised groups is characterised by everyday brute violence (instead of exceptional episodes of violence). Here, I am not aiming at a linear account of colonial continuities or continuities of enslavement. However, looking at the function of policing in the colonies and with regard to plantation economies can teach something about the relation between race, policing and intersectional forms of violence. As Simone Browne lays out in her important book on the relation between surveillance and blackness,[292] observation, routines and self-discipline as forms of **disciplinary power** are not the dominant forms of power blackness is subjected to. Rather, blackness is also subjected to everyday repressive and brute forms of violence, which continue to shape racialised experiences of policing and surveillance in (**formally**) postcolonial times.

EVERYDAY AND NORMALISED 'EXCEPTIONS'

Various community organisations and networks – including cop-watch collectives, human rights organisations and legal networks in many parts of the world – emphasise that everyday policing as a form of organised (silent and slow but also fast and loud) violence represents a normalised and, indeed, *everyday* experience for many vulnerable and racialised groups, especially along the intersections of class, gender, sexuality, migrant status and mental health. These experiences are normalised as they are often not seen or registered by dominant parts of society and represent the norm rather than an exception. Further, they are often **legitimised** as policing is embedded in societal forms of criminalisation so that dominant parts of society either do not see the violence in policing, or perceive policed subjects as criminal and hence as perpetrators and never as victims of violence – or both. In fact, what are often perceived as 'exceptions' or as 'individual cases' with regard to policing, such as incidents of police violence, represent an everyday experience for many marginalised people, especially members of multi-marginalised groups. Women and LGBT*IQ refugees/impoverished black people/ people of colour with disabilities and illegalised migrant sex workers are particularly vulnerable – as intersectional and abolitionist feminists remind us – to racist police controls, abuse and their various, sometimes deadly, consequences.[293]

Thus, policing draws on and shapes intersectional forms of violence, which means that subjects who experience interlocking forms of violence simultaneously (such as racism, migration regimes, hetero-patriarchy, ableism and economic deprivation) are particularly vulnerable to policing *and* experience policing alongside these dimensions of violence (such as the criminalisation of poor and racialised communities, sexualised and gendered violence against women and gender non-conforming folks and the pathologisation of **mad** folks and folks with disabilities) as the state produces these forms of violence constantly. Further, policing, as an institutionalised practice of control and punishment, interacts with related coercive institutions in an intersectional way (not only with the prison or the detention centre, but also with the foster care regime, the social welfare and housing system and psychiatric institutions). In her important work based on activism and legal support of black women, indigenous women and women of colour, *Invisible no More: Police Violence against Black Women and Women of Color,* Andrea J. Ritchie shows that policing is an everyday experience for racialised women and gender non-conforming folks in the US, who are brutalised along gender lines, often represented as promiscuous and read as sex workers, policed as mothers and left without protection (police in-action) as well as experiencing sexual assault and violence by police.[294] Jaime Amparo Alves discusses this in the context of Brazil.[295]

Recent scholarly and activist interventions have also highlighted the intersectional dimension of policing with regard to European contexts and show that being read as a sex worker and policed also manifests in the experiences of black women and queer folks in these contexts. For racialised sex workers, policing also manifests in further criminalisation and often devastating consequences with regard, for example, to child custody rights.[296] Further, fatal police killings also cost the lives of racialised women and **non-binary** folks as racial profiling does not end with stop and search controls.

In the German context, one can think of Christy Schwundeck, who was fatally shot in a job centre in Frankfurt am Main on May 19, 2011 while enquiring about her unemployment benefits. The case of N'deye Mariame Sarr, who was shot by police on July 14, 2001 in the house of her white ex-partner, is a further manifestation of how racism, gender relations, migrant status, social class and dis/ability intersect in policing.[297] In both cases, two or more police or security officers as well as one more person were present and Christy Schwundeck and N'deye Mariame Sarr were the only black women in these respective situations. Both were in a situation of crisis. Christy Schwundeck had been without money for over two weeks as her unemployment benefits had not arrived. N'deye Mariame Sarr wanted to pick up her two-year-old child from her white ex-partner, from whom she had separated. He had brought the child to his parents and applied for sole child custody without letting her know. Both shots were fired shortly after police arrived. Mariame Sarr was one of the first people to be shot by the new *PEP (Polizei-*

Einsatz-Patrone), a special bullet with a mushroom effect, created to gun down 'very violent attackers', a category that is often already inscribed and tattooed on black skin. In both instances, public prosecutors closed the case on the grounds of 'self-defence'.

I CAN'T BREATHE

Multi-marginalised groups experience policing as a condition of *un-breathing* in various but interrelated ways. I conceptualise un-breathing as a **material**, social and physical condition and experience. 'I can't breathe' were the last words of George Floyd. They were also the last words of Eric Garner, while being chocked to death on July 7, 2014 in New York. Kwaku Ofori in Finland remembers the last words of his friend Samuel Dolphyne as the following: 'He was shouting and calling my name; Ofori, Ofori they are killing me. I can't breathe.'[298] Wilson A. from Zurich, Switzerland was coming from meeting a friend when he was stopped and searched by police after a ticket control on a tram on October 10, 2009. He was aggressively pushed out of the tram and then brutally beaten after he asked why police had only controlled him and his friend. Wilson A. told the police that he'd just had heart surgery, but the police continued and even insulted him with racist slurs. As stated in the many reports of support groups and his own testimony, Wilson A. could barely breathe. Since 2009, he and his supporters have been fighting for justice. The fierce refugee activist Sista Mimi, who was engaged in the refugee protests at the Oranienplatz and the Gerhart-Hauptmann School in Berlin, died on December 11, 2014. During her long-term self-organised refugee and migrant activism, she continuously argued that the repression by police absorbed her breath.

Escaping stop and search controls, being on the move and on the run,[299] means to be out of breath. 'Breathing' refers to the physical as well as to the social breathing here. I approach these experiences through a Fanonian framework and follow, amongst others, the crucial and material condition of un-breathing, a motif that sticks to the policing of race, especially of blackness, and its intersectional dimensions through time and space. Fanon wrote that the colonial condition is characterised by 'combat breathing'.[300] Combat breathing is embodied in and through the pant for breath, the gasp for air, the compression of air supply, the chokehold, the panic attack. It refers to the loss of breath when you find out that you have lost a loved one through police violence, and while you struggle for a justice that is rarely achieved through the criminal justice system, as well as to the fear of being policed when going outside, in the grocery store, etc. It refers to the inhalation of water as in drowning as a result of the policing of the Black Mediterranean[301] and the systematic regimes of death-making at state borders. Policing as the condition of un-breathing endangers and renders impossible *life* for vulnerable groups all over the world. Policing as the historical and constant condition of un-breathing is the stuff out of which modern security and **subjectivity** is made in racial gendered capitalism.

ABOLITION

For centuries abolitionists have challenged and resisted regimes of punishment, surveillance, and organised violence by exposing the logics of racial gendered capitalism – from the abolition of enslavement to abolitionist anti-colonial struggles, from struggles against apartheid to struggles against systems of lynching and imprisonment. Policing, and the ways it relates to all of these, has been and is being challenged as a crucial component of abolition. But the various forms in which systems of oppression make us re-produce violence on interpersonal levels are also subjects of abolition. Twenty years ago, the anti-violence and abolitionist organisations *INCITE!* and *Critical Resistance*, both based in the US, wrote a statement that connects interpersonal to **structural violence** and urges us to centre vulnerable women, queer and non-binary folks in abolitionist struggles as they experience interpersonal as well as state violence, and movements that only address one of these levels reproduce violence on the other.[302] They called for social justice movements to address both state and interpersonal forms of violence, which are often closely linked as societal violence and abandonment creates the climate for interpersonal forms of violence to flourish. The statement shows that abolition must be intersectional in its understanding of, and resistance to, state violence and interpersonal violence, which unfold along intersectional dimensions, *as well as* intersectional in its understanding of institutions of violence, as state violence is produced and affirmed not only by policing but also by other state institutions and even non-state **agents**. These institutions (such as police, courts, job centres, hospitals, schools, private security companies, the foster care regime) often work in complex constellations and in concert in the production of intersectional violence through criminalisation and policing as a relation of control, through punishment or abandonment (or both).

But there are also examples of collectives and groups beyond the US that have developed intersectional and holistic approaches such as *Women in Exile, LesMigraS,* the *Transformative Justice Kollectiv* and various cop-watch collectives in Germany, *Sisters Uncut* in the UK, and *Reaja ou Será Morta, Reaja ou Será Morto* in Brazil, even if some of them do not refer to the term 'abolition' explicitly. Drawing on various methods such as community accountability and transformative justice as politics of care, which challenge all forms of violence, these and other collectives demonstrate in important ways that abolition is not just about getting rid of violent institutions or relations, but about building institutions and relations that stand in stark contrast to the politics of violence and death, as they render possible breathing and life.

Vanessa E. Thompson co-founded an intersectional cop-watch collective in Germany and was active in the Christy Schwundeck Initiative. She is a postdoctoral researcher and lecturer in comparative social and cultural anthropology at European University Viadrina, teaching and working in the fields of black studies, critical racism studies, postcolonial feminism and abolition.

NOTES

INTRODUCTION

---

1. Cops Off Campus, 'All Out To Tottenham (15th December 2013)'.

2. El-Enany, '"Innocence Charged with Guilt": The Criminalisation of Protest from Peterloo to Millbank'; Myers, *Student Revolt: Voices of the Austerity Generation*.

3. Barkas, 'Framing the Death of Mark Duggan.'

4. Lakhani, 'Judge Says Riot Sentences Were Fair'; The Guardian & London School of Economics (LSE), 'Reading the Riots: Investigating England's Summer of Disorder'.

5. Abolition University Studies, 'Cops Off Campus Database: Research Project [Toolkit - Beta Version]'.

6. Conn, 'Hillsborough Disaster: Deadly Mistakes and Lies That Lasted Decades'.

7. Shaw, 'Met Police Corruption Probe Papers Shredded "Over Two Days"'.

8. As I argue in Duff, 'The Criminal Is Political: Policing Politics in Real Existing Liberalism'.

9. This concept is well explained in Finlayson, *Introduction to Feminism*, chap. 3.

10. Long-time prison organiser John Bowden reflects on this in Woodman, '40 Years in Prison, 40 Years of Struggle: An Interview with John Bowden'. For a classic account of the phenomenon, see Fanon, *The Wretched of the Earth*.

11. Searcey and Eligon, 'Minneapolis Will Dismantle Its Police Force, Council Members Pledge'.

12. Duff and Woodman, 'We Must Abolish Police to Create a More Equal Society'.

13. Schrader, 'Rethinking Race and Policing in Imperial Perspective', 40–41.

14. Cited in Schrader, 40.

15. For more on this issue, see: Morrigan, *Fuck The Police Means We Don't Act Like Cops To Each Other* [Zine]; Wynn, 'Canceling| Contrapoints [Video]'.

16. Bureau of Public Secrets, 'May 1968 Graffiti'.

17. Wilson Gilmore, *Golden Gulag: Prisons, Surplus, Crisis, and Opposition in Globalizing California*, 28.

18. Bonney, *Letters Against the Firmament*, 141.

19. See the brilliant Graeber, 'On the Phenomenon of Bullshit Jobs: A Work Rant'.

20. ASBO: Anti-Social Behaviour Order.

21. Hartman, *Wayward Lives, Beautiful Experiments: Intimate Histories of Social Upheaval*, 74.

22. Hartman, 283–85.

23. For more on this idea, see: Rossdale, 'Dancing Ourselves To Death: The Subject of Emma Goldman's Nietzschean Anarchism'; Duff, 'Resisting Liberal Self-Deception'; Delmas, *A Duty to Resist: When Disobedience Should Be Uncivil.*

24. I discuss my case and issues around strip search abuse and the police complaints procedure in Duff, Ryder, and Swann, 'The Lockdown: Policing By Consent? [Podcast]'. I investigate the relation between sexual violence and policing more generally, analysing strip search practices as one example, in Duff, 'Feminism Against Crime Control: On Sexual Subordination and State Apologism'.

25. Reported in Lowbridge, '"Degrading Strip Search Left Me With PTSD"'.

26. For the meaning and origins of this phrase, see TV Tropes, 'Lie Back and Think of England'.

27. Duff and Kemp, 'Would "Defund the Police" Work in the UK?'

28. By this I mean the task of staying alive to the 'sparks of hope' contained in the past, in the 'tradition of the oppressed' – the ways that struggles and ideas and images thought long buried in the rubble of failure can 'flash up in a moment of danger' to speak to the needs of the present. I find these ideas in Benjamin, 'On the Concept of History'. See Leslie, 'Walter Benjamin: The Refugee and Migrant'.

29. All fragments in italics are from Bonney, *Happiness: Poems After Rimbaud* & *Letters Against the Firmament.*

MARTIAL POLITICS, POLICE POWER: ABOLITION, WAR AND THE ARMS TRADE

30. DSEI, 'Welcome to DSEI'.

31. Rossdale, *Resisting Militarism: Direct Action and the Politics of Subversion.*

32. Balko, *Rise of the Warrior Cop: The Militarization of America's Police Forces*; Wood, *Crisis and Control: The Militarization of Protest Policing.*

33. Howell, 'Forget "Militarization"': Race, Disability and the "Martial Politics" of the Police and of the University'.

34. Césaire, *Discourse on Colonialism*; Go, 'The Imperial Origins of American Policing: Militarization and Imperial Feedback in the Early 20th Century'.

35. Bloom and Martin, *Black against Empire: The History and Politics of the Black Panther Party*; Newton, *Revolutionary Suicide.*

36. Abu-Jamal, 'Frantz Fanon and His Influence on the Black Panther Party and the Black Revolution'; Malloy, *Out of Oakland: Black Panther Internationalism During the Cold War*, 18–45.

37. Cleaver, *Soul on Ice*, 164.

38. Newton, *Revolutionary Suicide*, 118.

39. Newton, *The Huey P. Newton Reader*, 173–88.

40. Narayan, 'The Wages of Whiteness in the Absence of Wages: Racial Capitalism, Reactionary Intercommunalism and the Rise of Trumpism'; Narayan, 'Huey P. Newton's Intercommunalism: An Unacknowledged Theory of Empire'.

41. Newton, *The Huey P. Newton Reader*, 187.

42. The national guard was mobilised to suppress an urban rebellion in Detroit in 1967, a task that, in concert with the police, state guard and army, they undertook with indiscriminate and deadly force (Bloom and Martin, *Black against Empire*, 86–91). The writings of Panther leader George Jackson, who was incarcerated in Soledad Prison, set out the racist and capitalist violence of the US prison system (Jackson, *Soledad Brother: The Prison Letters of George Jackson*). Jackson was killed during an escape attempt in 1971.

43. Newton, *The Huey P. Newton Reader*, 186.

44. Khalili, *Time in the Shadows: Confinement in Counterinsurgencies*; Neocleous, *War Power, Police Power*; Schrader, *Badges without Borders: How Global Counterinsurgency Transformed American Policing*.

45. Neocleous, *War Power, Police Power*, 9–15.

46. Neocleous, 10–11.

47. Bhattacharyya, *Rethinking Racial Capitalism: Questions of Reproduction and Survival*, 5.

48. Wang, *Carceral Capitalism*.

49. CAAT, 'What Is DSEI?'; Holden, *Indefensible: Seven Myths that Sustain the Global Arms Trade*.

WE ARE ALL POLICE NOW: RESISTING EVERYDAY BORDERING AND THE HOSTILE ENVIRONMENT

50. UK Government, 'Immigration Enforcement: Operation Vaken'.

51. Hattenstone, 'Why Was the Scheme behind May's "Go Home" Vans Called Operation Vaken?'

52. Travis, '"Go Home" Vans Resulted in 11 People Leaving Britain, Says Report'.

53. UK Government, 'Inspection Report on Illegal Working, December 2015'.

54. Syal, 'Immigration Officers Compete on Arrest Numbers to Win Cake – Union'.

55. Corporate Watch, 'UK Border Regime: Immigration Raids Briefing October 2018'.

56. Yuval-Davis, Wemyss, and Cassidy, 'Everyday Bordering, Belonging and the Reorientation of British Immigration Legislation'.

57. Kirkup, 'Theresa May Interview: "We're Going to Give Illegal Migrants a Really Hostile Reception"'.

58. UK Government, 'Immigration Act 2014'; UK Government, 'Immigration Act 2016'.

59. For a counter-example, see Haque, 'Britain Deports People Who Grew up Here. This Racialised System Must End'.

60. Shahvisi and Finnerty, 'Why It Is Unethical to Charge Migrant Women for Pregnancy Care in the National Health Service'.

61. Gentleman, 'Windrush Cancer Patient Has UK Residency Status Confirmed'.

62. Fourie, 'Moral Distress and Moral Conflict in Clinical Ethics'.

63. Shahvisi, 'Austerity or Xenophobia? The Causes and Costs of the "Hostile Environment" in the NHS'.

64. Dustmann and Frattini, 'The Fiscal Effects of Immigration to the UK'.

65. Shahvisi, 'The UK Must Stop Compelling Asylum Seekers to Risk Their Lives'.

66. Sabsay, 'The Emergence of the Other Sexual Citizen: Orientalism and the Modernisation of Sexuality'.

67. Becker, 'Crime and Punishment: An Economic Approach'.

68. Corporate Watch, 'UK Border Regime: Immigration Raids Briefing October 2018'.

69. Walsh, 'Migration to the UK: Asylum and Resettled Refugees'.

70. Tusalem, 'The Colonial Foundations of State Fragility and Failure'; McKeown, 'Who Bears Responsibility for Post-Colonial Poverty?'

71. Except those whose labour was required in building state institutions such as the NHS. See Shahvisi, 'Health Worker Migration and Migrant Healthcare: Seeking Cosmopolitanism in the NHS'.

72. See e.g. Southall Black Sisters, 'SBS Opposes Immigration Raid in Southall'.

73. BMA, 'BMA Says Charging Regulations for Overseas Patients Are Threatening the Quality of NHS Care'.

74. Docs Not Cops, Medact, and Migrants Organise.

WHY BORDERS *AND* PRISONS, BORDER GUARDS *AND* POLICE?

75. Brown, 'House of Commons Hansard Debates for 25 July 2007 (Pt 0004)'.

76. This has been slowly eroded through campaigning efforts in the last two years and has dramatically decreased as a response to Covid-19.

77. Infologue, 'Manned Security E-Zine – Operation Nexus Launches'.

78. Infologue.

79. De Noronha, 'Unpacking the Figure of the "Foreign Criminal": Race, Gender and the Victim-Villain Binary'; Griffiths, 'Foreign, Criminal: A Doubly Damned Modern British Folk-Devil'.

80. Mamdani, *Citizen and Subject: Contemporary Africa and the Legacy of Late Colonialism*.

81. Fernandez, 'The Geographies of Prevent: The Transformation of the Muslim Home into a Pre-Crime Space'; Goldberg, Jadhav, and Younis, 'Prevent: What is Pre-Criminal Space?'

82. Centre for Contemporary Cultural Studies, *EMPIRE STRIKES BACK: Race and Racism in 70s Britain*.

83. Bhambra, 'The Current Crisis of Europe: Refugees, Colonialism, and the Limits of Cosmopolitanism'.

84. El-Enany, *Bordering Britain: Law, Race and Empire*, ix.

85. Buxton and Akkerman, 'The Rise of Border Imperialism'.

86. Sinclair, 'Exporting the UK Police "Brand": The RUC-PSNI and the International Policing Agenda'.

87. Home Office, Great Britain, *Life in the United Kingdom*, 43.

88. Williams, *Capitalism and Slavery*; Bryan, *Heart Of The Race: Black Women's Lives in Britain*.

89. Doulton, '"The Flag That Sets Us Free": Antislavery, Africans, and the Royal Navy in the Western Indian Ocean'.

90. Buxton et al., *The African Slave Trade and Its Remedy*, 483.

91. Elliott-Cooper, 'When Did We Come to Britain? You Must Be Mistaken, Britain Came to Us'.

92. Tabili, 'The Construction of Racial Difference in Twentieth-Century Britain: The Special Restriction (Coloured Alien Seamen) Order, 1925'.

93. Jones, 'Butler's Colour-Bar Bill Mocks Commonwealth'.

94. Hunte, *N***er Hunting in England?*; Sivanandan, 'From Resistance to Rebellion: Asian and Afro-Caribbean Struggles in Britain', 119.

95. Ramamurthy, *Black Star: Britain's Asian Youth Movements*.

96. Bryan, *Heart Of The Race*.

97. This very brief survey of anti-racist movements does a disservice to a richer and more complicated historical picture that attends to divergent 'integrationist' and 'autonomous' approaches toward the police in anti-racist organising. See Ashe, Virdee, and Brown, 'Striking Back Against Racist Violence in the East End of London, 1968–1970'.

98. Nulman, 'Neo-Imperialism in Solidarity Organisations' Public Discourses'; Narayan and Sealey-Huggins, 'Whatever Happened to the Idea of Imperialism?'

99. Bhattacharyya, *Rethinking Racial Capitalism: Questions of Reproduction and Survival*.

100. Smith and Mac, *Revolting Prostitutes: The Fight for Sex Workers' Rights*.

101. Hall, *Policing the Crisis: Mugging, the State, and Law and Order*.

102. Duff and Kemp, 'Would "Defund the Police" Work in the UK?'

103. For a detailed study of the Reparations Movement see Beckles, *Britain's Black Debt: Reparations for Caribbean Slavery and Native Genocide*.

104. Wilson Gilmore, 'Abolition Geography and the Problem of Innocence'.

105. Bowling and Westenra, '"A Really Hostile Environment": Adiaphorization, Global Policing and the Crimmigration Control System'; Griffiths, 'Foreign, Criminal'.

106. BBC Panorama, *Undercover: Britain's Immigration Secrets*.

DEFENDING THE 'LIBERAL-DEMOCRATIC ORDER': THE STRATEGIC-POLITICAL LOGIC OF COUNTER-SUBVERSION

107. Quoted in Grierson, Dodd, and Walker, 'Putting Extinction Rebellion on Extremist List "Completely Wrong", Says Keir Starmer'.

108. Grierson and Dodd, 'Terrorism Police List Extinction Rebellion as Extremist Ideology'.

109. Grierson and Dodd, 'Terror Police List That Included Extinction Rebellion Was Shared across Government'.

110. Grierson and Dodd, 'Greenpeace Included with Neo-Nazis on UK Counter-Terror List'.

111. Grierson and Dodd, 'Greenpeace Included with Neo-Nazis on UK Counter-Terror List'.

112. Evans and Lewis, *Undercover: The True Story of Britain's Secret Police*.

113. Greenwald, 'How Covert Agents Infiltrate the Internet to Manipulate, Deceive, and Destroy Reputations'.

114. Casciani, 'Metropolitan Police Admits Role in Blacklisting Construction Workers'.

115. In the midst of an extensive analysis of intelligence overreach in the US, John Prados comments – without elaboration – that, 'Perhaps the most disturbing aspect of all is that Family Jewels [political intelligence scandals] seem to have a tendency to replicate, suggesting that abuse fulfils some functional purpose' (Prados, *The Family Jewels: The CIA, Secrecy and Presidential Power*, 322). Conservative military historian David French can readily admit that the role of colonial police in the British empire was 'protecting the economic and political interests of the colonial state, and ensuring the government was not overthrown' – but makes a categorical distinction with the domestic English police (French, *The British Way in Counter-Insurgency 1945-1967*, 17).

116. Rusche and Kirchheimer, *Punishment and Social Structure*.

117. Foucault, *Discipline and Punish: The Birth of the Prison*, 55.

118. Wilson, 'Extremism Rebellion: Review of Tactics and Ideology'.

119. BBC News, 'Stephen Lawrence Murder: Met Refuses Cdr Richard Walton Action'.

120. Walton, 'Preface', 5.

121. Walton, 6.

122. Maguire, 'Counter-Subversion in Early Cold War Britain: The Official Committee on Communism (Home), the Information Research Department, and "State-Private Networks"', 640–41.

123. MI5, 'FAQs about MI5'.

124. Porter, 'Other People's Mail'.

125. There are also several instances of sections of the intelligence agencies working to undermine elected Labour governments, notably during the 1924 Zinoviev Letter incident and the 1960s and 1970s 'Wilson Plots'. These, however, were carried out by rightist sections of the intelligence agencies and were largely *deviations* from their explicit constitutional role, the work of particular individuals and sub-organisational networks. Whether a genuinely socialist Labour government would be subject to a full-blown undermining by the entirety of the counter-subversion apparatus remains, however, to be seen. For more, see Woodman, 'Spycops in Context: A Brief History of Political Policing in Britain'.

126. Woodman, 'Spycops in Context: Counter-Subversion, Deep Dissent and the Logic of Political Policing'.

127. Finlayson, *The Political Is Political: Conformity and the Illusion of Dissent in Contemporary Political Philosophy*; Duff, 'The Criminal Is Political: Policing Politics in Real Existing Liberalism', 486.

128. Woodman, 'Spycops in Context: Why Does the State Infiltrate Political Organisations?'

129. Bunyan, *The History and Practice of the Political Police in Britain*, 108.

130. Evans and Lewis, *Undercover: The True Story of Britain's Secret Police*, 150–67.

131. Elliott-Cooper, 'Violence Old and New: From Slavery to Serco'.

132. Thomson, *Queer People*, 273.

133. Thomson, 266.

134. Chomsky, 'Domestic Terrorism: Notes on the State System of Oppression'.

135. Shiraishi, 'A New Regime of Order: The Origin of Modern Surveillance Politics in Indonesia', 55.

136. Cobain, '"Subversive" Civil Servants Secretly Blacklisted under Thatcher'.

137. Bunyan, *The History and Practice of the Political Police in Britain*, 138.

138. Marx, 'Thoughts on a Neglected Category of Social Movement Participant: The Agent Provocateur and the Informant'.

139. Woodman, 'Spycops in Context: A Brief History of Political Policing in Britain', 13–15.

140. Milne, *The Enemy Within: The Secret War Against the Miners*.

141. Loosened from the necessity of adhering to the rules of successful prosecution, undercover police are allowed far greater scope for creative interpretations of the regulations governing surveillance, as a former undercover police officer has noted (Woods, 'Exposing Undercover Policing in The U.K.').

142. Channel 4, *Cutting Edge: Confessions of an Undercover Cop*.

143. Loadenthal, 'When Cops "Go Native": Policing Revolution through Sexual Infiltration and Panopticonism'.

144. Foucault, *Discipline and Punish: The Birth of the Prison*, 94–95.

145. For example, Bob Lambert, of the Special Demonstration Squad, who allegedly carried out a firebombing of a Debenhams store in the 1980s whilst undercover in the Animal Liberation Front (Evans and Lewis, *Undercover: The True Story of Britain's Secret Police*, 26–44), or Freddie Scappaticci, a police and Force Research Unit (military intelligence) informer in the IRA who executed

numerous other UK agents with the go-ahead from the British state in order to protect his identity (BBC Panorama, *The Spy in the IRA*).

FROM THE COLONY TO THE METROPOLE: RACE, POLICING AND THE COLONIAL BOOMERANG

146. Bell, 'Normalising the Exceptional: British Colonial Policing Cultures Come Home'.

147. Césaire, *Discourse on Colonialism*, 36; see also Woodman, 'The Imperial Boomerang: How Colonial Methods of Repression Migrate Back to the Metropolis'.

148. Padmore, *How Britain Rules Africa*, 4.

149. Brogden, 'The Emergence of the Police—The Colonial Dimension'; also see Cohen, 'Policing the Working Class City'.

150. Brogden, 9.

151. Taylor, *Brits: The War Against the IRA*.

152. This author considers "Northern Ireland" (the North of the Republic of Ireland) to be a British settler colony and will therefore place it in double inverted commas throughout the piece.

153. Meiksins Wood, *Empire of Capital*.

154. Wolfe, *Traces of History: Elementary Structures of Race*.

155. Said, *Orientalism*.

156. Ellison and Smyth, *The Crowned Harp: Policing Northern Ireland*.

157. Hillyard, *Suspect Community: People's Experience of the Prevention of Terrorism Acts in Britain*.

158. Bell, 'Normalising the Exceptional'.

159. Ellison and O'Reilly, 'From Empire to Iraq and the "War on Terror": The Transplantation and Commodification of the (Northern) Irish Policing Experience'.

160. Hillyard, 'Policing Divided Societies: Trends and Prospects in Northern Ireland and Britain.'

161. Gilroy, 'The Myth of Black Criminality'.

162. Reiner, *The Politics of the Police*, 68.

163. Green, *Cities Under Siege: The New Military Urbanism*.

164. Green, xvii.

165. Chowdhury, Minott, and Williams, 'Unfair Criminalisation of Moss Side Residents'.

166. Gilroy, *There Ain't No Black in the Union Jack*, 91.

167. Hall, *Policing the Crisis: Mugging, the State, and Law and Order*.

168. Gilroy, *There Ain't No Black in the Union Jack*; see also Chowdhury, 'Policing the Black Party'.

169. Clarke and Williams, 'Dangerous Associations: Joint Enterprise, Gangs and Racism'; Williams, 'Being Matrixed: The (over)Policing of Gang Suspects in London.'

170. Dodd, 'Met Police Push Ahead with Armed Patrols Despite Backlash'.

171. Baxter, 'Police Use of Force Statistics, England and Wales April 2018 to March 2019'.

172. Baxter.

173. Blowe, 'The Rise of Militarised Policing'.

174. Boher, Fabian, and Castro, 'A People's History of Police Exchanges: Settler Colonialism, Capitalism and the Intersectionality of Struggles'.

STATUES AND GANGS: FASCIST PANIC AND POLICING

175. Clowes, '"You're Antifa!" [Video]'.

176. Burton et al., 'Talking Colston: Memory, Commemoration and Bristol's Slave Legacy'.

177. Mukerjee, *Churchill's Secret War: The British Empire and the Ravaging of India During WWII.*

178. Gayle, 'Boris Johnson Condemns "Racist Thuggery" of Rightwing Protesters in London'.

179. Reuters, 'Boris Johnson: Anti-Racism Protests "Subverted by Thuggery"'.

180. Ministry of Justice, 'Criminal Justice Statistics Quarterly, England and Wales'.

181. Farrell, *Crime, Class and Corruption: Politics of the Police*; Moore, 'Is the Empire Coming Home? Liberalism, Exclusion and the Punitiveness of the British State'.

182. Moore.

183. Wilson Gilmore and Petitjean, 'Prisons and Class Warfare: An Interview with Ruth Wilson Gilmore'.

184. Hall, *Policing the Crisis: Mugging, the State, and Law and Order.*

185. Williams, 'From Muggers to Gangs, It's the Same Police Story'.

186. Williams.

187. Dodd, 'Cressida Dick Appointed First Female Met Police Commissioner'.

188. Quoted in Gayle, 'Anti-Fascists Block Route of Democratic Football Lads Alliance London March'.

189. Gebrial, 'The Far Right Don't Care about Sexual Violence – They're Just Trying to Gain Political Power'.

190. Jay, 'Independent Inquiry into Child Sexual Exploitation in Rotherham'.

191. Goodfellow, *Hostile Environment: How Immigrants Became Scapegoats*.

192. Perraudin, 'Judges Uphold Decision to Strip Grooming Gang Members of Citizenship'.

193. Webber, 'The Embedding of State Hostility: A Background Paper on the Windrush Scandal'.

194. Lammy, 'Lammy Review: Final Report, An Independent Review into the Treatment of, and Outcomes for, Black, Asian and Minority Ethnic Individuals in the Criminal Justice System'.

195. Phillips, 'High Police Support for Greece's Golden Dawn'.

196. Kreuzer, *'If They Resist, Kill Them All': Police Vigilantism in the Philippines*.

197. Kreuzer.

BLACK LIVES AND THE STATE OF DISTRACTION

198. Morrison, 'Black Studies Center Public Dialogue. Pt. 2'.

199. Wilson Gilmore, *Golden Gulag: Prisons, Surplus, Crisis, and Opposition in Globalizing California*, 28.

200. Williams, *The Alchemy of Race and Rights: Diary of a Law Professor*.

POLICE ABOLITION AND RADICAL DEMOCRACY

201. Benjamin, 'Critique of Violence', 251–52. Translation modified.

202. See Loick, 'Was ist Polizeikritik?'

203. Benjamin, 'Critique of Violence', 287.

204. Muir, *Police: Streetcorner Politicians*.

205. Lipsky, *Toward a Theory of Street-Level Bureaucracy*.

206. Fassin, 'Discretionary Power and Security Politics: Grey Cheque from the State to the Police'.

207. Thompson, '"Hey, Sie da!" Postkolonial-feministische Kritik der Polizei am Beispiel von Racial Profiling'.

208. Baldwin, 'A Report from Occupied Territory'; Taylor, *From #BlackLivesMatter to Black Liberation*, chap. 4.

209. Guenther, 'Seeing Like a Cop: A Critical Phenomenology of Whiteness as Property'.

210. Friedersdorf, 'Police Have a Much Bigger Domestic-Abuse Problem than the NFL Does'.

211. Hall, *Policing the Crisis: Mugging, the State, and Law and Order*.

212. Wacquant, *Punishing the Poor: The Neoliberal Government of Social Insecurity*.

213. Davis, *Are Prisons Obsolete?*; Wilson Gilmore, *Golden Gulag: Prisons, Surplus, Crisis, and Opposition in Globalizing California*.

214. On the history of the BPP, see: Jefferies, *The Black Panther Party in A City Near You*; Joseph, *Neighborhood Rebels: Black Power at the Local Level*; Spencer, *The Revolution Has Come: Black Power, Gender, and the Black Panther Party in Oakland*; Williams and Lazerow, *Liberated Territories: Untold Local Perspectives on the Black Panther Party*.

215. Loick, 'Rechtskritik und Abolitionismus. Die Rechtstheorie der Black Panthers'.

216. Young, 'The Logic of Masculinist Protection: Reflections on the Current Security State'.

217. Communities Against Rape and Abuse (CARA), 'Taking Risks: Implementing Grassroots Community Accountability Strategies'; generationFIVE, 'Ending Child Sexual Abuse: A Transformative Justice Handbook'; Kaba and Brooks, 'Whose Security Is It Anyway? A Toolkit to Address Institutional Violence in Non-Profit Organizations'; Dixon and Piepzna-Samarasinha, *Beyond Survival: Strategies and Stories from the Transformative Justice Movement*.

218. Du Bois, *Black Reconstruction in America, 1860-1880*, 184–85.

219. Dilts, 'Crisis, Critique, and Abolition', 234.

220. Dilts, 247.

221. Davis, *Abolition Democracy: Beyond Empire, Prisons, and Torture*, 96.

222. Davis, 103.

223. Loick, 'Law Without Violence'; Loick, *A Critique of Sovereignty*, pt. III.

224. Benjamin, 'Critique of Violence', 244.

225. Habermas, *Between Facts and Norms: Contributions to a Discourse Theory of Law and Democracy*, 8.

226. For an overview, see Williams, *Our Enemies in Blue: Police and Power in America*; Taylor, *From #BlackLivesMatter to Black Liberation*; McLeod, 'Envisioning Abolition Democracy: Developments in the Law'.

227. Benjamin, 'Critique of Violence', 243.

POLICING AND COERCION: WHAT ARE THE ALTERNATIVES?

228. Locke, *Political Essays*, 129. This brief account of Locke is deliberately stylised for the purposes of highlighting one of the more prominent liberal strategies for justifying coercive authority. A full account of Locke's discussion of the state of nature would need to stress his justification of private property rights and processes of accumulation, for which see Macpherson, *The Political Theory of Possessive Individualism*.

229. See Connor Woodman's chapter in this collection.

230. See e.g. Balko, *Rise of the Warrior Cop: The Militarization of*

America's Police Forces, and Chris Rossdale's chapter in this collection.

231. See e.g. Gilmore and Tufail, 'Justice Denied: Police Accountability and the Killing of Mark Duggan'.

232. This means projecting normative concepts (such as 'rights') from our own society into an imagined future in ways that some emancipatory theorists, following Marx, have been sceptical about. There are important concerns here to do with the danger of importing conceptual frameworks that merely reproduce existing power relations. I tend to think these concerns are important, though not decisive, as I discuss here: Aitchison, 'Are Human Rights Moralistic?'

233. Rossi and Sleat, 'Realism in Normative Political Theory'.

234. See the chapter on radical democracy by Daniel Loick in this volume.

235. This sometimes happens in cases of civil disobedience. See, for instance, Chakravarti, 'Edward Snowden Deserves to Be Tried By a Jury of His Peers, Just Like Everyone Else'.

PRACTISING EVERYDAY ABOLITION

236. Wilson Gilmore and Lambert, 'Making Abolition Geography in California's Central Valley with Ruth Wilson Gilmore'.

237. Angela Davis, *Are Prisons Obsolete?*

238. Wilson Gilmore and Murakawa, 'Covid-19, Decarceration, and Abolition [Webinar]'.

239. As Berger, Kaba and Stein describe them, non-reformist reforms are 'measures that reduce the power of an oppressive system while illuminating the system's inability to solve the crises

it creates.' For an example in relation to policing, see Critical Resistance, 'Reformist Reforms vs. Abolitionist Steps in Policing [Abolitionist Reforms Chart]'. For UK version see Abolitionist Futures, 'Defund the Police [Infographics]'.

240. Berger, Kaba, and Stein, 'What Abolitionists Do'.

241. Graham et al., 'School Exclusion: A Literature Review on the Continued Disproportionate Exclusion of Certain Children'.

242. Community United Against Violence (CUAV), 'Gems of Change: Pendulum of Approaches'.

243. generationFIVE, 'Ending Child Sexual Abuse: A Transformative Justice Handbook'; Simmons, *Love WITH Accountability: Digging Up the Roots of Child Sexual Abuse*.

244. Gossett, Spade, and Dector, 'No One Is Disposable: Everyday Practices of Prison Abolition'.

245. Creative Interventions, 'Creative Interventions Toolkit: A Practical Guide to Stop Interpersonal Violence'.

246. For a definition of transformative justice, see Bay Area Transformative Justice Collective, 'Transformative Justice and Community Accountability'.

247. Moss, 'Love-Centred Accountability'.

248. Dixon and Piepzna-Samarasinha, *Beyond Survival: Strategies and Stories from the Transformative Justice Movement*.

249. Creative Interventions, 'Creative Interventions Toolkit: A Practical Guide to Stop Interpersonal Violence'.

250. Hollaback, 'Resources'.

251. Russo, *Feminist Accountability: Disrupting Violence and Transforming Power*.

252. Russo, '10 Strategies for Cultivating Community Accountability'.

253. Simmons, 'Love WITH Accountability: A Mother's Lament'; Moss, 'Love-Centred Accountability'.

254. Russo, '10 Strategies for Cultivating Community Accountability'.

255. Cheng Thom, 'What to Do When You've Been Abusive', 69.

256. See for example the work done by groups like: Creative Interventions; generationFIVE; INCITE! Women of Color Against Violence; Project NIA; Bay Area Transformative Justice Collective; Sex Worker Advocacy and Resistance Movement (SWARM); DIY Space for London; Transformative Justice Kollectiv, Berlin; and the resource hub TransformHarm.org.

257. Kaba, 'Transform Harm Resource Hub'; Rose, 'What to Do Instead of Calling the Police'; Amezcua, Dixon, and Long, 'Ten Lessons for Creating Safety Without Police'; Dixon and Piepzna-Samarasinha, *Beyond Survival*.

258. Moore, 'Love Is a Reckoning', 3.

259. Dixon, 'Building Community Safety: Practical Steps Toward Liberatory Transformation', 21.

260. Community United Against Violence (CUAV), 'Our Analysis of Violence'.

THEORIZING TRANSFORMATIVE JUSTICE: COMPARING CARCERAL AND ABOLITIONIST SELVES, AGENCIES, AND RESPONSIBILITIES

261. Spade, 'Their Laws Will Never Make Us Safer: An Introduction', 6.

262. INCITE!, 'INCITE! Women of Color Against Violence Community Accountability Principles/Concerns/Strategies/Models Working Document', 1.

263. Bernstein, 'The Sexual Politics of the "New Abolitionism"'; Kim, 'Dancing the Carceral Creep: The Anti-Domestic Violence Movement and the Paradoxical Pursuit of Criminalization, 1973 – 1986'; Law, 'Against Carceral Feminism'; Richie, *Arrested Justice: Black Women, Violence, and America's Prison Nation.*

264. INCITE!, *Color of Violence: The INCITE! Anthology*; Ritchie, *Invisible No More: Police Violence Against Black Women and Women of Color.*

265. Ritchie, 'How Some Cops Use the Badge to Commit Sex Crimes'; Cheema, 'Black and Blue Bloods'.

266. Crenshaw, 'From Private Violence to Mass Incarceration: Thinking Intersectionally About Women, Race, and Social Control'.

267. Critical Resistance and INCITE!, 'The Critical Resistance INCITE! Statement on Gender Violence and the Prison Industrial Complex'.

268. Chen, Dulani, and Piepzna-Samarasinha, *The Revolution Starts at Home: Confronting Intimate Violence within Activist Communities;*

Creative Interventions, 'Creative Interventions Toolkit: A Practical Guide to Stop Interpersonal Violence (Pre-Release Version)'; Kershnar et al., 'Toward Transformative Justice. A Liberatory Approach to Child Sexual Abuse and Other Forms of Intimate and Community Violence. A Call to Action for the Left and the Sexual and Domestic Violence Sectors.'

269. INCITE!, 'Community Accountability Fact Sheet'.

270. Dixon and Piepzna-Samarasinha, *Beyond Survival: Strategies and Stories from the Transformative Justice Movement.*

271. Young, *Responsibility for Justice.*

272. Hudson, 'Punishing the Poor: Dilemmas of Justice and Difference', 192.

273. Creative Interventions, 'Creative Interventions Toolkit: A Practical Guide to Stop Interpersonal Violence (Pre-Release Version)', 1:5.

274. Brown, 'Wounded Attachments'.

275. Bierria, 'Missing in Action: Violence, Power, and Discerning Agency', 137.

276. Bierria, 130.

277. Bierria, 132.

278. Augusta-Scott, 'Letters from Prison: Reauthoring Identity With Men Who Have Perpetrated Sexual Violence'.

279. Brown, 'Wounded Attachments'.

280. Boodman, 'An Immanent Critique of the Prison Nation: The Contradictions of Carceral "Anti-Violence"'.

281. Brown, *Politics Out of History*, 10.

282. See, for example, Burk, 'Think. Re-Think. Accountable Communities'.

BEYOND POLICING, FOR A POLITICS OF BREATHING

283. Wilson Gilmore, *Golden Gulag: Prisons, Surplus, Crisis, and Opposition in Globalizing California*.

284. Diaz, 'Police Handcuff Black Doctor Who Tests Homeless for Coronavirus'.

285. In the following, I write 'case', 'example' or 'incident' when referring to experiences of policing, while knowing that these words actually fail to express what is at stake. Lived experiences of violence always entail more than reductive and quantifying terms such as 'examples' or 'cases' can capture.

286. See Benjamin, 'Black Skin, White Masks: Racism, Vulnerability & Refuting Black Pathology'.

287. Collectif urgence notre police assassine, 'Les familles, les militants et artistes appellent à télécharger l'application UVP.'

288. Miren, 'The English Collective of Prostitutes: Occupation of Holy Cross Church'.

289. Purnell, 'Coronavirus Has Shown That It Is Possible to Change the US Criminal Justice System'.

290. Davis, *Abolition Democracy: Beyond Empire, Prisons, and Torture*; Ritchie, *Invisible No More: Police Violence Against Black Women and Women of Color*; Maynard, *Policing Black Lives: State Violence in Canada from Slavery to the Present*.

291. Fanon, *The Wretched of the Earth*, 38.

292. Browne, *Dark Matters: On the Surveillance of Blackness*.

293. Bruce-Jones, 'German Policing at the Intersection: Race, Gender, Migrant Status and Mental Health'; Dankwa, Ammann, and dos Santos Pinto, 'Profiling und Rassismus im Kontext von Sexarbeit'; Kollaborative Forschungsgruppe, *Racial Profiling. Erfahrung, Wirkung, Widerstand*. Maynard, *Policing Black Lives: State Violence in Canada from Slavery to the Present*; Ritchie, *Invisible No More: Police Violence Against Black Women and Women of Color*; Thompson, '"Hey, Sie da!" Postkolonial-feministische Kritik der Polizei am Beispiel von Racial Profiling'.

294. Ritchie, *Invisible No More*.

295. Alves, *The Anti-Black City: Police Terror and Black Urban Life in Brazil*.

296. Dankwa, Ammann, and dos Santos Pinto, 'Profiling und Rassismus im Kontext von Sexarbeit'.

297. Bruce-Jones, 'German Policing at the Intersection: Race, Gender, Migrant Status and Mental Health'.

298. GH Diaspora, 'UPDATE: Austrian Based Ghanaian Dies in the Hands of Police in Finland'.

299. See Traoré and de Lagasnerie, *Le combat Adama – Les Essais*.

300. Fanon, *A Dying Colonialism*.

301. Smythe, 'The Black Mediterranean and the Politics of Imagination'.

302. Critical Resistance and INCITE!, 'The Critical Resistance INCITE! Statement on Gender Violence and the Prison Industrial Complex'.

BIBLIOGRAPHY

Abolition University Studies. 2020. 'Cops Off Campus Database: Research Project [Toolkit - Beta Version]'. *Abolition University*. Accessed 14 November 2020.

Abolitionist Futures. 2020. 'Defund the Police [Infographics]'. *Abolitionist Futures*. Accessed 14 November 2020.

Abu-Jamal, Mumia. 2019. 'Frantz Fanon and His Influence on the Black Panther Party and the Black Revolution'. In *Frantz Fanon and Emancipatory Social Theory*, edited by Dustin J. Byrd and Seyed Javad. Boston, MA: Brill.

Aitchison, Guy. 2018. 'Are Human Rights Moralistic?' *Human Rights Review* 19 (1): 23–43.

Alves, Jaime Amparo. 2018. *The Anti-Black City: Police Terror and Black Urban Life in Brazil*. Minneapolis, MN: University of Minnesota Press.

Amezcua, Tasha, Ejeris Dixon, and Che J. Rene Long. 2016. 'Ten Lessons for Creating Safety Without Police'. *Truthout.org*. 14 July 2016.

Ashe, Stephen, Satnam Virdee, and Laurence Brown. 2016. 'Striking Back Against Racist Violence in the East End of London, 1968–1970'. *Race & Class* 58 (1): 34–54.

Augusta-Scott, Tod. 2006. 'Letters from Prison: Reauthoring Identity With Men Who Have Perpetrated Sexual Violence'. In *Narrative Therapy: Making Meaning, Making Lives*, edited by Catrina Brown and Tod Augusta-Scott, 251–68. SAGE Publications.

Baldwin, James. 1966. 'A Report from Occupied Territory'. *The Nation*, 1966.

Balko, Radley. 2013. *Rise of the Warrior Cop: The Militarization of America's Police Forces*. New York: PublicAffairs.

Barkas, Betsy. 2014. 'Framing the Death of Mark Duggan'. *Institute of Race Relations*, 14 April 2014. Accessed 14 January 2021.

Baxter, Amy. 2019. 'Police Use of Force Statistics, England and Wales April 2018 to March 2019'. Home Office. *Gov.uk*.

Bay Area Transformative Justice Collective. 2013. 'Transformative Justice and Community Accountability'. <https://batjc.files.wordpress.com/2014/06/tj-ca-one-pager.pdf> Accessed 1 May 2020.

BBC News. 2016. 'Stephen Lawrence Murder: Met Refuses Cdr Richard Walton Action'. *BBC News*, 20 January 2016.

BBC Panorama. 2017a. *The Spy in the IRA*. *BBC One*, 18 April 2017.

———. 2017b. *Undercover: Britain's Immigration Secrets*. *BBC One*, 9 September 2017.

Becker, Gary S. 1968. 'Crime and Punishment: An Economic Approach'. In *The Economic Dimensions of Crime*, 13–68. Springer.

Beckles, Hilary McD. 2012. *Britain's Black Debt: Reparations for Caribbean Slavery and Native Genocide*. Kingston, Jamaica: University of West Indies Press.

Bell, Emma. 2013. 'Normalising the Exceptional: British Colonial Policing Cultures Come Home'. *Mémoire(s), identité(s), marginalité(s) dans le monde occidental contemporain*, 10.

Benjamin, Ruha. 2020. 'Black Skin, White Masks: Racism, Vulnerability & Refuting Black Pathology'. *Princeton University, Department of African American Studies* [departmental blog], 15 April 2020.

Benjamin, Walter. 1986. 'Critique of Violence'. First published 1921 in German. In *Reflections*. New York: Schocken.

———. 2006. 'On the Concept of History'. In *Walter Benjamin: Selected Writings, Volume 4: 1938-1940*, edited by Howard Eiland and Michael W. Jennings, translated by Edmund Jephcott, 389–400. Cambridge, MA: Belknap Press of Harvard University Press.

Berger, Dan, Mariame Kaba, and David Stein. 2017. 'What Abolitionists Do'. *Jacobin Magazine*, 24 August 2017.

Bernstein, Elizabeth. 2007. 'The Sexual Politics of the "New Abolitionism"'. *Differences: A Journal of Feminist Cultural Studies* 18 (3): 128–51.

Bhambra, Gurminder K. 2017. 'The Current Crisis of Europe: Refugees, Colonialism, and the Limits of Cosmopolitanism'. *European Law Journal* 23 (5): 395–405.

Bhattacharyya, Gargi. 2018. *Rethinking Racial Capitalism: Questions of Reproduction and Survival*. Cultural Studies and Marxism. Lanham, MD: Rowman & Littlefield.

Bierria, Alisa. 2014. 'Missing in Action: Violence, Power, and Discerning Agency'. *Hypatia* 29 (1): 129–45.

Bloom, Joshua, and Waldo E Martin. 2013. *Black against Empire: The History and Politics of the Black Panther Party*. Oakland, CA: University of California Press.

Blowe, Kevin. 2016. 'The Rise of Militarised Policing'. *Red Pepper Magazine*, 20 January 2016.

BMA. 2019. 'BMA Says Charging Regulations for Overseas Patients Are Threatening the Quality of NHS Care'. 18 April 2019. Accessed 24 April 2020.

Boher, Ashley, Andres Fabian, and Henao Castro. 2019. 'A People's History of Police Exchanges: Settler Colonialism, Capitalism and the Intersectionality of Struggles'. In *The War on Drugs and the Global Colour Line*, edited by Kojo Koram. London: Pluto Press.

Bonney, Sean. 2011. *Happiness: Poems After Rimbaud*. London: Unkant Publishing.

———. 2015. *Letters Against the Firmament*. London: Enitharmon Press.

Boodman, Eva. 2018. 'An Immanent Critique of the Prison Nation: The Contradictions of Carceral "Anti-Violence"'. *Philosophy & Social Criticism* 44 (5): 571–592.

Bowling, Ben, and Sophie Westenra. 2018. '"A Really Hostile Environment": Adiaphorization, Global Policing and the Crimmigration Control System:' *Theoretical Criminology* 24 (2).

Brogden, Mike. 1987. 'The Emergence of the Police—The Colonial Dimension'. *The British Journal of Criminology* 27 (1).

Brown, Gordon. 2007. 'House of Commons Hansard Debates for 25 July 2007 (Pt 0004)'. Accessed 10 June 2020.

Brown, Wendy. 1993. 'Wounded Attachments'. *Political Theory* 21 (3): 390–410.

———. 2001. *Politics Out of History*. Princeton, NJ: Princeton University Press.

Browne, Simone. 2015. *Dark Matters: On the Surveillance of Blackness*. Durham, NC: Duke University Press.

Bruce-Jones, Eddie. 2015. 'German Policing at the Intersection: Race, Gender, Migrant Status and Mental Health'. *Race and Class* 56 (3): 36–49.

Bryan, Beverley. 1985. *Heart Of The Race: Black Women's Lives in Britain*. 1st paperback edition. London: Virago.

Bunyan, Tony. 1977. *The History and Practice of the Political Police in Britain*. London: Quartet Books.

Bureau of Public Secrets. 'May 1968 Graffiti'. *Bureau of Public Secrets* <http://www.bopsecrets.org/CF/graffiti.htm> Accessed 23 December 2020

Burk, Connie. 2011. 'Think. Re-Think. Accountable Communities'. In *The Revolution Starts at Home: Confronting Intimate Violence within Activist Communities*, edited by Ching-In Chen, Jai Dulani, and Leah Lakshmi Piepzna-Samarasinha, 265–80. Brooklyn, NY: South End Press.

Burton, Edson, Madge Dresser, Francis Greenacre, and Olivette Otele. 2016. 'Talking Colston: Memory, Commemoration and Bristol's Slave Legacy'. Presented at the The BIRTHA Annual Debates, The Station, Bristol, 5 May 2016.

Buxton, Nick, and Mark Akkerman. 2018. 'The Rise of Border Imperialism'. *ROAR Magazine*, no. 8 (Summer 2018).

Buxton, Thomas Fowell, Wendell Phillips, William Lloyd Garrison, and Society for the Extinction of the Slave Trade and for the Civilization of Africa. 1840. *The African Slave Trade and Its Remedy*. London: John Murray.

CAAT. 2019. 'What Is DSEI?' *Campaign Against The Arms Trade*. Accessed 23 December 2020.

Casciani, Dominic. 2018. 'Metropolitan Police Admits Role in Blacklisting Construction Workers'. *BBC News,* 23 March 2018.

Centre for Contemporary Cultural Studies. 1982. *EMPIRE STRIKES BACK: Race and Racism in 70's Britain.* London: Routledge.

Césaire, Aimé. 2001. *Discourse on Colonialism.* First published 1955 in French. New edition. Translated by Joan Pinkham, edited by Robin D. G. Kelly. New York: Monthly Review Press.

Chakravarti, Sonali. 2019. 'Edward Snowden Deserves to Be Tried By a Jury of His Peers, Just Like Everyone Else'. *The Nation*, 9 October 2019.

Channel 4. 2011. *Cutting Edge: Confessions of an Undercover Cop.* 14 November 2011.

Cheema, Rafaqat. 2016. 'Black and Blue Bloods: Protecting Police Officer Families from Domestic Violence'. *Family Court Review* 54 (3): 487–500.

Chen, Ching-In, Jai Dulani, and Leah Lakshmi Piepzna-Samarasinha, eds. 2011. *The Revolution Starts at Home: Confronting Intimate Violence within Activist Communities.* Brooklyn, NY: South End Press.

Cheng Thom, Kai. 2020. 'What to Do When You've Been Abusive'. In *Beyond Survival: Strategies and Stories from the Transformative Justice Movement*, edited by Ejeris Dixon and Leah Lakshmi Piepzna-Samarasinha, 74–87. Chico, CA: AK Press.

Chomsky, Noam. 1999. 'Domestic Terrorism: Notes on the State System of Oppression'. *New Political Science* 21 (3): 303–24.

Chowdhury, Tanzil. 2019. 'Policing the Black Party'. In *The War on Drugs and the Global Colour Line*, edited by Kojo Koram. London: Pluto Press.

Chowdhury, Tanzil, Akemia Minott, and Patrick Williams. 2017. 'Unfair Criminalisation of Moss Side Residents'. *The Guardian*, 27 February 2017.

Clarke, Becky, and Patrick Williams. 2015. 'Dangerous Associations: Joint Enterprise, Gangs and Racism'. *Centre for Crime and Justice Studies.*

Cleaver, Eldridge. 1968. *Soul on Ice.* Repr. A Delta Book. New York: Dell Publishing.

Clowes, Ed (@EdClowes). 2020. '"You're Antifa!" [Video]'. Twitter, 13 June 2020, 2:55 p.m. <https://twitter.com/EdClowes/status/1271803498653458434> Accessed 23 December 2020.

Cobain, Ian. 2018. '"Subversive" Civil Servants Secretly Blacklisted under Thatcher'. *The Guardian*, 24 July 2018.

Cohen, Phil. 1979. 'Policing the Working Class City'. In *Capitalism and the Rule of Law: From Deviancy to Marxism*, edited by Bob Fine, Richard Kinsey, John Lea, Sol Picciotto and Jack Young, 118–36. London: Hutchinson.

Collectif urgence notre police assassine. 2020. 'Les familles, les militants et artistes appellent à télécharger l'application UVP'. *Facebook*, 24 April 2020. Accessed 23 December 2020.

Communities Against Rape and Abuse (CARA). 2017. 'Taking Risks: Implementing Grassroots Community Accountability Strategies'. In *Color of Violence: The INCITE! Anthology.* Durham, NC: Duke University Press.

Community United Against Violence (CUAV). 2013. 'Gems of Change: Pendulum of Approaches'. *Everyday Abolition / Abolition Every Day,* 11 July 2013.

———. 2019. 'Our Analysis of Violence'. *CUAV*. Accessed 23 December 2020.

Conn, David. 2016. 'Hillsborough Disaster: Deadly Mistakes and Lies That Lasted Decades'. *The Guardian*, 26 April 2016.

Cops Off Campus. 2015. 'All Out To Tottenham (15th December 2013)'. In *Bad Feelings*, an Arts Against Cuts collection, designed and edited by Sophie Carapetian, Louis Hartnoll, Robyn Minogue, Lucy Killoran, and Nina Power. London: Book Works.

Corporate Watch. 2018. 'UK Border Regime: Immigration Raids Briefing October 2018'. *Corporate Watch*, 26 October 2018.

Creative Interventions. 2012. 'Creative Interventions Toolkit: A Practical Guide to Stop Interpersonal Violence (Pre-Release Version)'.

———. 2020. 'Creative Interventions Toolkit: A Practical Guide to Stop Interpersonal Violence'. *Creative Interventions,* 1 May 2020. Accessed 23 December 2020.

Crenshaw, Kimberlé W. 2012. 'From Private Violence to Mass Incarceration: Thinking Intersectionally About Women, Race, and Social Control'. *UCLA Law Review* 59: 1418–72.

Critical Resistance. 2020. 'Reformist Reforms vs. Abolitionist Steps in Policing [Abolitionist Reforms Chart]'. 1 May 2020. Accessed 23 December 2020.

Critical Resistance, and INCITE! 2001. 'The Critical Resistance INCITE! Statement on Gender Violence and the Prison Industrial Complex'. *INCITE!* Accessed 23 December 2020.

Dankwa, Serena, Christa Ammann, and Jovita dos Santos Pinto. 2019. 'Profiling und Rassismus im Kontext von Sexarbeit'. *Racial Profiling. Struktureller Rassismus und Antirassistischer Widerstand* 31: 155–71.

Davis, Angela. 2003. *Are Prisons Obsolete?* New York: Seven Stories.

———. 2005. *Abolition Democracy: Beyond Empire, Prisons, and Torture.* New York City: Seven Stories Press.

De Noronha, Luke. 2015. 'Unpacking the Figure of the "Foreign Criminal": Race, Gender and the Victim-Villain Binary'. *Centre on Migration, Policy, and Society (COMPAS)*, University of Oxford.

Delmas, Candice. 2018. *A Duty to Resist: When Disobedience Should Be Uncivil.* Oxford: Oxford University Press.

Diaz, Johnny. 2020. 'Police Handcuff Black Doctor Who Tests Homeless for Coronavirus'. *New York Times*, 14 April 2020.

Dilts, Andrew. 2019. 'Crisis, Critique, and Abolition'. In *A Time for Critique*, edited by Didier Fassin and Bernard Harcourt. New York: Columbia University Press.

Dixon, Ejeris. 2020. 'Building Community Safety: Practical Steps Toward Liberatory Transformation'. In *Beyond Survival: Strategies and Stories from the Transformative Justice Movement*, edited by Ejeris Dixon and Leah Lakshmi Piepzna-Samarasinha, 14–24. Chico, CA: AK Press.

Dixon, Ejeris, and Leah Lakshmi Piepzna-Samarasinha. 2020. *Beyond Survival: Strategies and Stories from the Transformative Justice Movement.* Chico, CA: AK Press.

Dodd, Vikram. 2017. 'Cressida Dick Appointed First Female Met Police Commissioner'. *The Guardian*, 22 February 2017.

———. 2018. 'Met Police Push Ahead with Armed Patrols Despite Backlash'. *The Guardian*, 1 December 2018.

Doulton, Lindsay. 2013. '"The Flag That Sets Us Free": Antislavery, Africans, and the Royal Navy in the Western Indian Ocean'. In *Indian Ocean Slavery in the Age of Abolition*, edited by Robert Harms, Bernard K. Freamon, and David W. Blight, 101–19. New Haven, CT: Yale University Press.

DSEI. 2020. 'Welcome to DSEI'. *DSEI.co.uk*. Accessed 23 December 2020.

Du Bois, W. E. B. 1998. *Black Reconstruction in America, 1860-1880*. First published 1935. New York: The Free Press.

Duff, Koshka. 2017. 'The Criminal Is Political: Policing Politics in Real Existing Liberalism'. *Journal of the American Philosophical Association* 3 (4): 485–502.

———. 2018. 'Feminism Against Crime Control: On Sexual Subordination and State Apologism'. *Historical Materialism* 26 (2): 123–46.

———. 2019. 'Resisting Liberal Self-Deception'. *European Journal of Philosophy* 27: 1075–83.

Duff, Koshka, and Tom Kemp. 2020. 'Would "Defund the Police" Work in the UK?' *Novara Media*, 15 June 2020.

Duff, Koshka, and Connor Woodman. 2020. 'We Must Abolish Police to Create a More Equal Society'. *Huck Magazine*, 12 October 2020.

Duff, Koshka, Oonagh Ryder, and Sam Swann. 2018. 'The Lockdown: Policing by Consent? [Podcast]'. *Novara Media*, 30 November 2018.

Dustmann, Christian, and Tommaso Frattini. 2014. 'The Fiscal Effects of Immigration to the UK'. *The Economic Journal* 124 (580): F593–643.

El-Enany, Nadine. 2014. '"Innocence Charged with Guilt": The Criminalisation of Protest from Peterloo to Millbank'. In *Riots, Unrest and Protest on the Global Stage*, edited by David Pritchard and Frances Pakes, 72–97. London: Palgrave Macmillan.

———. 2020. *Bordering Britain: Law, Race and Empire*. Manchester: Manchester University Press.

Elliott-Cooper, Adam. 2015. 'When Did We Come to Britain? You Must Be Mistaken, Britain Came to Us'. *Verso*, 20 October 2015.

———. 2019. 'Violence Old and New: From Slavery to Serco'. In *Blackness in Britain*, edited by Kehinde Andrews and Lisa Amanda Palmer, 76–86. London: Routledge.

Ellison, Graham, and Conor O'Reilly. 2008. 'From Empire to Iraq and the "War on Terror": The Transplantation and Commodification of the (Northern) Irish Policing Experience'. *Police Quarterly* 11 (4).

Ellison, Graham, and Jim Smyth. 2000. *The Crowned Harp: Policing Northern Ireland*. London: Pluto Press.

Evans, Rob, and Paul Lewis. 2013. *Undercover: The True Story of Britain's Secret Police*. London: Faber and Faber.

Fanon, Frantz. 1965. *A Dying Colonialism*. New York: Grove Press.

———. 2004. *The Wretched of the Earth*. First published 1961 in French. Translated by Richard Philcox. New York: Grove Press.

Farrell, Audrey. 1995. *Crime, Class and Corruption: The Politics of the Police*. Reprint. First published 1992. London: Bookmarks.

Fassin, Didier. 2014. 'Discretionary Power and Security Politics: Grey Cheque from the State to the Police'. *Actes de la recherche en sciences sociales* 201–202 (1): 72–86.

Fernandez, Shereen. 2018. 'The Geographies of Prevent: The Transformation of the Muslim Home into a Pre-Crime Space'. *Journal of Muslims in Europe* 7 (June): 167–89.

Finlayson, Lorna. 2015. *The Political Is Political: Conformity and the Illusion of Dissent in Contemporary Political Philosophy*. London: Rowman & Littlefield.

———. 2016. *Introduction to Feminism*. Cambridge: Cambridge University Press.

Foucault, Michel. 1977. *Discipline and Punish: The Birth of the Prison*. First published 1975 in French. Translated by Alan Sheridan. New York: Vintage Books.

Fourie, Carina. 2015. 'Moral Distress and Moral Conflict in Clinical Ethics'. *Bioethics* 29 (2): 91–97.

French, David. 2011. *The British Way in Counter-Insurgency 1945-1967*. Oxford: Oxford University Press.

Friedersdorf, Conor. 2014. 'Police Have a Much Bigger Domestic-Abuse Problem than the NFL Does'. *The Atlantic*, 9 September 2014.

Gayle, Damien. 2018. 'Anti-Fascists Block Route of Democratic Football Lads Alliance London March'. *The Guardian*, 13 October 2018.

———. 2020. 'Boris Johnson Condemns "Racist Thuggery" of Rightwing Protesters in London'. *The Guardian*, 13 June 2020.

Gebrial, Dalia. 2018. 'The Far Right Don't Care about Sexual Violence – They're Just Trying to Gain Political Power'. *Novara Media*, 1 December 2018.

generationFIVE. 2018. 'Ending Child Sexual Abuse: A Transformative Justice Handbook'. *generationFIVE,* 23 January 2018. Accessed 23 December 2020.

Gentleman, Amelia. 2018. 'Windrush Cancer Patient Has UK Residency Status Confirmed'. *The Guardian*, 27 April 2018.

GH Diaspora, 'UPDATE: Austrian Based Ghanaian Dies in the Hands of Police in Finland'. 2018. *GH Diaspora*, 21 November 2018.

Gilmore, Joanna, and Waqas Tufail. 2015. 'Justice Denied: Police Accountability and the Killing of Mark Duggan'. In *How Corrupt Is Britain?*, edited by David Whyte. London: Pluto Press.

Gilroy, Paul. 1982. 'The Myth of Black Criminality'. *Socialist Register*.

———. 2002. *There Ain't No Black in the Union Jack*. 2nd edition. London: Routledge.

Go, Julian. 2020. 'The Imperial Origins of American Policing: Militarization and Imperial Feedback in the Early 20th Century'. *American Journal of Sociology* 125 (5): 1193–1254.

Goldberg, David, Sushrut Jadhav, and Tarek Younis. 2017. 'Prevent: What Is Pre-Criminal Space?' *BJPsych Bulletin* 41 (4): 208–11.

Goodfellow, Maya. 2019. *Hostile Environment: How Immigrants Became Scapegoats*. London: Verso.

Gossett, Reina, Dean Spade, and Hope Dector. 2020. 'No One Is Disposable: Everyday Practices of Prison Abolition'. *Barnard Centre for Research on Women*, 1 May 2020.

Graeber, David. 2013. 'On the Phenomenon of Bullshit Jobs: A Work Rant'. *STRIKE! Magazine*, August 2013.

Graham, Berni, Clarissa White, Amy Edwards, Sylvia Potter, and Cathy Street. 2019. 'School Exclusion: A Literature Review on the Continued Disproportionate Exclusion of Certain Children'. UK Department of Education. *Gov.uk*, May 2019.

Green, Stephen. 2010. *Cities Under Siege: The New Military Urbanism*. London: Verso.

Greenwald, Glenn. 2020. 'How Covert Agents Infiltrate the Internet to Manipulate, Deceive, and Destroy Reputations'. *The Intercept*, 24 February 2020.

Grierson, Jamie, and Vikram Dodd. 2020a. 'Terrorism Police List Extinction Rebellion as Extremist Ideology'. *The Guardian*, 10 January 2020.

————. 2020b. 'Greenpeace Included with Neo-Nazis on UK Counter-Terror List'. *The Guardian*, 17 January 2020.

————. 2020c. 'Terror Police List That Included Extinction Rebellion Was Shared across Government'. *The Guardian*, 27 January 2020.

Grierson, Jamie, Vikram Dodd, and Peter Walker. 2020. 'Putting Extinction Rebellion on Extremist List "Completely Wrong", Says Keir Starmer'. *The Guardian*, 13 January 2020.

Griffiths, Melanie. 2017. 'Foreign, Criminal: A Doubly Damned Modern British Folk-Devil'. *Citizenship Studies* 21 (5): 527–46.

Guenther, Lisa. 2019. 'Seeing Like a Cop: A Critical Phenomenology of Whiteness as Property'. In *Race as Phenomena: Between Phenomenology and Philosophy of Race*, edited by Emily Lee. London: Rowman & Littlefield.

Habermas, Jurgen. 1996. *Between Facts and Norms: Contributions to a Discourse Theory of Law and Democracy*. London: Palgrave MacMillan.

Hall, Stuart. 1978. *Policing the Crisis: Mugging, the State, and Law and Order*. Critical Social Studies. London: Macmillan.

Haque, Zubaida. 2019. 'Britain Deports People Who Grew up Here. This Racialised System Must End'. *The Guardian*, 11 February 2019.

Hartman, Saidiya. 2019. *Wayward Lives, Beautiful Experiments: Intimate Histories of Social Upheaval*. London: Serpent's Tail.

Hattenstone, Simon. 2018. 'Why Was the Scheme behind May's "Go Home" Vans Called Operation Vaken?' *The Guardian*, 26 April 2018.

Hillyard, Paddy. 1993. *Suspect Community: People's Experience of the Prevention of Terrorism Acts in Britain*. London: Pluto Press.

———. 1997. 'Policing Divided Societies: Trends and Prospects in Northern Ireland and Britain.' In *Policing Futures*, edited by Pamela Davis, Peter Francis, and Victor Jupp, 163–85.

Holden, Paul, ed. 2017. *Indefensible: Seven Myths That Sustain the Global Arms Trade*. London: Zed Books.

Hollaback. 2020. 'Resources'. *Hollaback!* Accessed 23 December 2020.

Home Office, Great Britain. 2014. *Life in the United Kingdom: A Guide for New Residents*. London: The Stationery Office.

Howell, Alison. 2018. 'Forget "Militarization": Race, Disability and the "Martial Politics" of the Police and of the University'. *International Feminist Journal of Politics*, 20(2): 1–20.

Hudson, Barbara. 2000. 'Punishing the Poor: Dilemmas of Justice and Difference'. In *From Social Justice to Criminal Justice: Poverty and the Administration of Criminal Law*, edited by William C. Heffernan and John Kleinig, 189–216. Oxford: Oxford University Press.

Hunte, Joseph A. 1966. *N***er Hunting in England?* London: West Indian Standing Conference (London Region).

INCITE! 2003. 'INCITE! Women of Color Against Violence Community Accountability Principles/Concerns/Strategies/Models Working Document'. *INCITE!* Accessed 23 December 2020.

———, ed. 2006. *Color of Violence: The INCITE! Anthology*. Cambridge, MA: South End Press.

———. 2008. 'Community Accountability Fact Sheet'. In *Law Enforcement Violence Against Women of Color and Trans People of Color: A Critical Intersection of Gender Violence and State Violence. An Organizer's Resource and Toolkit.*, 69–70. Redmond, WA: INCITE!

Infologue. 2012. 'Manned Security E-Zine — Operation Nexus Launches'. *Infologue.com.* <https://www.infologue.com/industry/operation-nexus-launches/>

Jackson, George. 1994. *Soledad Brother: The Prison Letters of George Jackson.* Chicago, IL: Lawrence Hill Books.

Jay, Alexis. 2014. 'Independent Inquiry into Child Sexual Exploitation in Rotherham'. Rotherham Metropolitan Borough Council. *Gov.uk.*

Jefferies, Judson, ed. 2018. *The Black Panther Party in A City Near You.* Atlanta, GA: University of Georgia Press.

Jones, Claudia. 2016. 'Butler's Colour-Bar Bill Mocks Commonwealth'. *Race & Class* 58 (1): 118–21.

Joseph, Peniel. 2010. *Neighborhood Rebels: Black Power at the Local Level.* London: Palgrave MacMillan.

Kaba, Mariame. 2020. 'Transform Harm Resource Hub'. *Transform Harm.* Accessed 23 December 2020.

Kaba, Mariame, and Lara Brooks. 2017. 'Whose Security Is It Anyway? A Toolkit to Address Institutional Violence in Non-Profit Organizations'. Available through *Survey Monkey.* Accessed 23 December 2020.

Kershnar, Sarah, Staci Haines, Gillian Harkins, Alan Greig, Cindy Wiesner, Mich Levy, Palak Shah, Mimi Kim, and Jesse Carr. 2007. 'Toward Transformative Justice. A Liberatory Approach to Child Sexual Abuse and Other Forms of Intimate and Community Violence. A Call to Action for the Left and the Sexual and Domestic Violence Sectors.' *generationFIVE.* Accessed 23 December 2020.

Khalili, Laleh. 2013. *Time in the Shadows: Confinement in Counterinsurgencies.* Stanford, CA: Stanford University Press.

Kim, Mimi Eunmi. 2014. 'Dancing the Carceral Creep: The Anti-Domestic Violence Movement and the Paradoxical Pursuit of Criminalization, 1973 – 1986'. Dissertation. Berkeley, CA.

Kirkup, James. 2012. 'Theresa May Interview: "We're Going to Give Illegal Migrants a Really Hostile Reception"'. *The Telegraph,* 25 May 2012.

Kollaborative Forschungsgruppe. 2019. *Racial Profiling. Erfahrung, Wirkung, Widerstand.* Berlin: Rosa Luxemburg Stiftung.

Kreuzer, Peter. 2016. *'If They Resist, Kill Them All': Police Vigilantism in the Philippines.* PRIF Report 142. Frankfurt am Main: Peace Research Institute Frankfurt.

Lakhani, Nina. 2012. 'Judge Says Riot Sentences Were Fair'. *The Independent*, 19 June 2012.

Lammy, David. 2017. 'Lammy Review: Final Report, An Independent Review into the Treatment of, and Outcomes for, Black, Asian and Minority Ethnic Individuals in the Criminal Justice System'. *Gov.uk.*

Law, Victoria. 2014. 'Against Carceral Feminism'. *Jacobin Magazine*, 17 October 2014.

Leslie, Esther. 2019. 'Walter Benjamin: The Refugee and Migrant'. *Verso*, 15 July 2019. First published 2015.

Lipsky, Michael. 1969. *Toward a Theory of Street-Level Bureaucracy.* Madison, WI: University of Wisconsin Press.

Loadenthal, Michael. 2014. 'When Cops "Go Native": Policing Revolution through Sexual Infiltration and Panopticonism'. *Critical Studies on Terrorism* 7 (1): 24–42.

Locke, John. 1997. *Political Essays.* Edited by Mark Goldie. Cambridge: Cambridge University Press.

Loick, Daniel. 2018a. 'Law Without Violence'. In *Law and Violence. Christoph Menke in Dialogue*, edited by Christoph Menke. Manchester: Manchester University Press.

—————. 2018b. 'Was ist Polizeikritik?' In *Kritik der Polizei*, edited by Daniel Loick. Frankfurt am Main/New York: Campus.

—————. 2019a. *A Critique of Sovereignty*. Translated by Amanda deMarco. London/New York: Rowman & Littlefield.

—————. 2019b. 'Rechtskritik und Abolitionismus. Die Rechtstheorie der Black Panthers'. *Juridikum. Zeitschrift für Kritik, Recht, Gesellschaft* 3: 384–95.

Lowbridge, Caroline. 2018. '"Degrading Strip Search Left Me With PTSD"'. *BBC News*, 22 October 2018.

Macpherson, C. B. 1962. *The Political Theory of Possessive Individualism: Hobbes to Locke*. Oxford: Clarendon Press.

Maguire, Thomas. 2015. 'Counter-Subversion in Early Cold War Britain: The Official Committee on Communism (Home), the Information Research Department, and "State-Private Networks"'. *Intelligence and National Security* 30 (5): 637–66.

Malloy, Sean L. 2017. *Out of Oakland: Black Panther Party Internationalism during the Cold War*. Ithaca, NY: Cornell University Press.

Mamdani, Mahmood. 1996. *Citizen and Subject: Contemporary Africa and the Legacy of Late Colonialism*. Princeton, NJ: Princeton University Press.

Marx, Gary T. 1974. 'Thoughts on a Neglected Category of Social Movement Participant: The Agent Provocateur and the Informant'. *American Journal of Sociology* 80 (2): 402–42.

Maynard, Robyn. 2017. *Policing Black Lives: State Violence in Canada from Slavery to the Present*. Black Point, NS: Fernwood Publishing.

McKeown, Maeve. 2011. 'Who Bears Responsibility for Post-Colonial Poverty?' Paper presented at *Princeton Graduate Political Theory Conference*.

McLeod, Allegra. 2019. 'Envisioning Abolition Democracy: Developments in the Law'. *Harvard Law Review*, 1613–49.

Meiksins Wood, Ellen. 2017. *Empire of Capital*. London: Verso.

MI5. 2020. 'FAQs about MI5'. *Gov.uk*, 16 April 2020. Accessed 23 December 2020.

Milne, Seamus. 2013. *The Enemy Within: The Secret War Against the Miners*. London: Verso.

Ministry of Justice. 2020. 'Criminal Justice Statistics Quarterly, England and Wales'. *Gov.uk*. Accessed 23 December 2020.

Miren, Frankie. 2020. 'The English Collective of Prostitutes: Occupation of Holy Cross Church'. *The British Library*, 20 October 2020.

Moore, Darnell L. 2019. 'Love Is a Reckoning'. In *Love WITH Accountability: Digging Up the Roots of Child Sexual Abuse*, edited by Aishah Shahida Simmons, 3–5. Chico, CA: AK Press.

Moore, John. 2014. 'Is the Empire Coming Home? Liberalism, Exclusion and the Punitiveness of the British State'. *Papers from the British Criminology Conference*, 14:31–48.

Morrigan, Clementine. 2020. *Fuck The Police Means We Don't Act Like Cops To Each Other* [Zine]. Tiohtià:ke/Montréal.

Morrison, Toni. 1975. 'Black Studies Center Public Dialogue. Pt. 2'. *Special Collections: Oregon Public Speakers*. 90.

Moss, Danielle R. 2019. 'Love-Centred Accountability'. In *Love WITH Accountability: Digging Up the Roots of Child Sexual Abuse*, edited by Aishah Shahida Simmons, 97–100. Chico, CA: AK Press.

Muir, William Kerr. 1977. *Police: Streetcorner Politicians*. Chicago, IL: University of Chicago Press.

Mukerjee, Madhusree. 2010. *Churchill's Secret War: The British Empire and the Ravaging of India during World War II*. New York: Basic Books.

Myers, Matt. 2017. *Student Revolt: Voices of the Austerity Generation*. London: Pluto Press.

Narayan, John. 2017. 'The Wages of Whiteness in the Absence of Wages: Racial Capitalism, Reactionary Intercommunalism and the Rise of Trumpism'. *Third World Quarterly* 38 (11): 2482–2500.

———. 2019. 'Huey P. Newton's Intercommunalism: An Unacknowledged Theory of Empire'. *Theory, Culture & Society* 36 (3): 57–85.

Narayan, John, and Leon Sealey-Huggins. 2017. 'Whatever Happened to the Idea of Imperialism?' *Third World Quarterly* 38 (11): 2387–95.

Neocleous, Mark. 2014. *War Power, Police Power*. Edinburgh: Edinburgh University Press.

Newton, Huey P. 2009. *Revolutionary Suicide*. Penguin Classics Deluxe Edition. New York: Penguin Books.

———. 2019. *The Huey P. Newton Reader*. Edited by David Hilliard, Donald Weise, and Elaine Brown. 2nd edition. New York: Seven Stories Press.

Nulman, Eugene. 2017. 'Neo-Imperialism in Solidarity Organisations' Public Discourses: Collective Action Frames, Resources and Audiences'. *Third World Quarterly* 38 (11): 2464–81.

Padmore, George. 1969. *How Britain Rules Africa*. Negro Universities Press.

Perraudin, Frances. 2018. 'Judges Uphold Decision to Strip Grooming Gang Members of Citizenship'. *The Guardian*, 8 August 2018.

Phillips, Barnaby. 2012. 'High Police Support for Greece's Golden Dawn'. *Al Jazeera Blog*, 20 December 2012.

Piepzna-Samarasinha, Leah Lakshmi, and Ejeris Dixon, eds. 2020. *Beyond Survival: Strategies and Stories from the Transformative Justice Movement*. Chico, CA: AK Press.

Porter, Bernard. 2009. 'Other People's Mail'. *London Review of Books Online*, 19 November 2009.

Prados, John. 2013. *The Family Jewels: The CIA, Secrecy and Presidential Power*. Austin, TX: University of Texas Press.

Purnell, Derecka. 2020. 'Coronavirus Has Shown That It Is Possible to Change the US Criminal Justice System'. *The Guardian*, 7 April 2020.

Ramamurthy, Anandi. 2013. *Black Star: Britain's Asian Youth Movements*. London: Pluto Press.

Reiner, Robert. 2019. *The Politics of the Police*. 3rd edition. Oxford: Oxford University Press.

Reuters. 2020. 'Boris Johnson: Anti-Racism Protests "Subverted by Thuggery"'. *BBC News*, 8 June 2020.

Richie, Beth E. 2012. *Arrested Justice: Black Women, Violence, and America's Prison Nation*. New York: New York University Press.

Ritchie, Andrea J. 2017. *Invisible No More: Police Violence Against Black Women and Women of Color*. Boston, MA: Beacon Press.

———. 2018. 'How Some Cops Use the Badge to Commit Sex Crimes'. *Washington Post*, 12 January 2018.

Rose, Aaron. 2018. 'What to Do Instead of Calling the Police'. *United Against Police Terror: San Diego*. Accessed 23 December 2020.

Rossdale, Chris. 2014. 'Dancing Ourselves to Death: The Subject of Emma Goldman's Nietzschean Anarchism'. *Globalizations* 12 (1): 116–33.

———. 2019. *Resisting Militarism: Direct Action and the Politics of Subversion*. Advances in Critical Military Studies. Edinburgh: Edinburgh University Press.

Rossi, Enzo, and Matt Sleat. 2014. 'Realism in Normative Political Theory'. *Philosophy Compass* 9 (10): 689–701.

Rusche, Georg, and Otto Kirchheimer. 2003. *Punishment and Social Structure*. Edited by Dario Melossi. First published 1939. London: Taylor & Francis.

Russo, Ann. 2013. '10 Strategies for Cultivating Community Accountability'. *US Prison Culture*, 16 September 2013. Accessed 23 December 2020.

———. 2018. *Feminist Accountability: Disrupting Violence and Transforming Power*. New York: New York University Press.

Sabsay, Leticia. 2012. 'The Emergence of the Other Sexual Citizen: Orientalism and the Modernisation of Sexuality'. *Citizenship Studies* 16 (5–6): 605–623.

Said, Edward. 1978. *Orientalism*. London: Penguin.

Schrader, Stuart. 2019. 'Rethinking Race and Policing in Imperial Perspective'. In *Badges Without Borders: How Counterinsurgency Transformed American Policing*. Oakland, CA: University of California Press.

———. 2019. *Badges Without Borders: How Counterinsurgency Transformed American Policing*. Oakland, CA: University of California Press.

Searcey, Dionne, and John Eligon. 2020. 'Minneapolis Will Dismantle Its Police Force, Council Members Pledge'. *New York Times*, 7 June 2020.

Shahvisi, Arianne. 2018. 'Health Worker Migration and Migrant Healthcare: Seeking Cosmopolitanism in the NHS'. *Bioethics* 32 (6): 334–42.

———. 2019. 'Austerity or Xenophobia? The Causes and Costs of the "Hostile Environment" in the NHS'. *Health Care Analysis* 27: 202–219.

———. 2020. 'The UK Must Stop Compelling Asylum Seekers to Risk Their Lives'. *International Observatory of Human Rights* [Blog], 22 May 2020. Accessed 23 December 2020.

Shahvisi, Arianne, and Fionnuala Finnerty. 2019. 'Why It Is Unethical to Charge Migrant Women for Pregnancy Care in the National Health Service'. *Journal of Medical Ethics*. 45 (8): 489–496.

Shaw, Danny. 2014. 'Met Police Corruption Probe Papers Shredded "Over Two Days"'. *BBC News*, 18 March 2014.

Shiraishi, Takashi. 2003. 'A New Regime of Order: The Origin of Modern Surveillance Politics in Indonesia'. In *Southeast Asia over Three Generations: Essays Presented to Benedict R. O'G. Anderson*. Ithaca, NY: Cornell Southeast Asia Program Publications.

Simmons, Aishah Shahida. 2019. *Love WITH Accountability: Digging Up the Roots of Child Sexual Abuse*. Chico, CA: AK Press.

Simmons, Gwendoyn Zohorah. 2019. 'Love WITH Accountability: A Mother's Lament'. In *Love WITH Accountability: Digging Up the Roots of Child Sexual Abuse*, edited by Aishah Shahida Simmons, 23–29. Chico, CA: AK Press.

Sinclair, Georgina. 2012. 'Exporting the UK Police "Brand": The RUC-PSNI and the International Policing Agenda'. *Policing: A Journal of Policy and Practice* 6 (1): 55–66.

Sivanandan, A. 1981. 'From Resistance to Rebellion: Asian and Afro-Caribbean Struggles in Britain'. *Race & Class* 22 (2–3): 111–52.

Smith, Molly, and Juno Mac. 2018. *Revolting Prostitutes: The Fight for Sex Workers' Rights.* London/New York: Verso.

Smythe, SA. 2018. 'The Black Mediterranean and the Politics of Imagination'. *Middle East Report* 286: 3–9.

Southall Black Sisters. 2013. 'SBS Opposes Immigration Raid in Southall'. *Southall Black Sisters* [Blog], 2013. Reposted 24 December 2020. Accessed 27 December 2020.

Spade, Dean. 2012. 'Their Laws Will Never Make Us Safer: An Introduction'. In *Against Equality: Prisons Will Not Protect You*, edited by Ryan Conrad, 1–12. Against Equality Press.

Spencer, Robyn. 2016. *The Revolution Has Come: Black Power, Gender, and the Black Panther Party in Oakland.* Durham, NC: Duke University Press.

Syal, Rajeev. 2018. 'Immigration Officers Compete on Arrest Numbers to Win Cake – Union'. *The Guardian*, 14 June 2018.

Tabili, Laura. 1994. 'The Construction of Racial Difference in Twentieth-Century Britain: The Special Restriction (Coloured Alien Seamen) Order, 1925'. *Journal of British Studies* 33 (1): 54–98.

Taylor, Keeanga-Yamahtta. 2016. *From #BlackLivesMatter to Black Liberation.* Chicago, IL: Haymarket Books.

Taylor, Peter. 2001. *Brits: The War Against the IRA.* London: Bloomsbury.

The Guardian & London School of Economics (LSE). 2011. 'Reading the Riots: Investigating England's Summer of Disorder'. *LSE Research Online.*

Thompson, Vanessa E. 2018. '"Hey, Sie da!" Postkolonial-feministische Kritik der Polizei am Beispiel von Racial Profiling'. In *Kritik der Polizei*, edited by Daniel Loick, 197–219. Frankfurt am Main/New York: Campus.

Thomson, Basil. 1922. *Queer People*. London: Hodder & Stoughton.

Traoré, Assa, and Geoffroy de Lagasnerie. 2019. *Le combat Adama – Les Essais*. Paris: Stock.

Travis, Alan. 2013. '"Go Home" Vans Resulted in 11 People Leaving Britain, Says Report'. *The Guardian*, 31 October 2013.

Tusalem, Rollin F. 2016. 'The Colonial Foundations of State Fragility and Failure'. *Polity* 48 (4): 445–495.

TV Tropes, n.d. 'Lie Back and Think of England'. *TV Tropes*. Accessed 19 December 2020.

UK Government. 2013. 'Immigration Enforcement: Operation Vaken'. *Gov.uk*, 31 October 2013. Accessed 23 December 2020.

———. 2014. 'Immigration Act 2014'. Queen's Printer of Acts of Parliament. 2014.

———. 2015. 'Inspection Report on Illegal Working, December 2015'. *Gov.uk*, 17 December 2015.

———. 2016. 'Immigration Act 2016'. Queen's Printer of Acts of Parliament. 2016.

Wacquant, Loïc. 2009. *Punishing the Poor: The Neoliberal Government of Social Insecurity*. Durham, NC: Duke University Press.

Walsh, Peter William. 2019. 'Migration to the UK: Asylum and Resettled Refugees'. *Migration Observatory*, 8 November 2019. Accessed 24 April 2020.

Walton, Richard. 2019. 'Preface'. In 'Extremism Rebellion: Review of Tactics and Ideology'. *Policy Exchange*.

Wang, Jackie. 2018. *Carceral Capitalism*. South Pasadena, CA: Semiotext(e).

Webber, Frances. 2018. 'The Embedding of State Hostility: A Background Paper on the Windrush Scandal'. Briefing paper 11. *Institute of Race Relations.*

Williams, Eric Eustace. 1964. *Capitalism and Slavery*. London: Andre Deutsch.

Williams, Johuru, and Jama Lazerow, eds. 2008. *Liberated Territories: Untold Local Perspectives on the Black Panther Party*. Durham, NC: Duke University Press.

Williams, Kristian. 2015. *Our Enemies in Blue: Police and Power in America*. Oakland, CA: AK Press.

Williams, Patricia. 1991. *The Alchemy of Race and Rights: Diary of a Law Professor*. Cambridge, MA: Harvard University Press.

Williams, Patrick. 2018a. 'Being Matrixed: The (over)Policing of Gang Suspects in London.' *Stopwatch: Research and Actions for Fair and Inclusive Policing*, August 2018.

———. 2018b. 'From Muggers to Gangs, It's the Same Police Story'. *Red Pepper Magazine*, 9 August 2018.

Wilson Gilmore, Ruth. 2007. *Golden Gulag: Prisons, Surplus, Crisis, and Opposition in Globalizing California*. Oakland, CA: University of California Press.

———. 2017. 'Abolition Geography and the Problem of Innocence'. In *Futures of Black Radicalism*, edited by Gaye Theresa Johnson and Alex Lubin, 216–35. London: Verso.

Wilson Gilmore, Ruth, and Clement Petitjean. 2018. 'Prisons and Class Warfare: An Interview with Ruth Wilson Gilmore'. *Verso*, 2 August 2018.

Wilson Gilmore, Ruth, and Léopold Lambert. 2019. 'Making Abolition Geography in California's Central Valley with Ruth

Wilson Gilmore'. *The Funambulist* 21 (Jan-Feb).

Wilson Gilmore, Ruth, and Naomi Murakawa. 2020. 'Covid-19, Decarceration, and Abolition [Webinar]'. *Youtube*, 28 April 2020 (event took place April 16).

Wilson, Tom. 2019. 'Extremism Rebellion: Review of Tactics and Ideology'. *Policy Exchange*.

Wolfe, Patrick. 2016. *Traces of History: Elementary Structures of Race*. London: Verso.

Wood, Lesley J. 2014. *Crisis and Control: The Militarization of Protest Policing*. London: Pluto Press.

Woodman, Connor. 2018a. 'Spycops in Context: A Brief History of Political Policing in Britain'. *Centre for Crime and Justice Studies*.

———. 2018b. 'Spycops in Context: Counter-Subversion, Deep Dissent and the Logic of Political Policing'. *Centre for Crime and Justice Studies*.

———. 2019. 'The Imperial Boomerang: How Colonial Methods of Repression Migrate Back to the Metropolis'. *Verso*, 22 July 2019.

———. 2020a. '40 Years in Prison, 40 Years of Struggle: An Interview with John Bowden'. *Novara Media,* 19 November 2020.

———. 2020b. 'Spycops in Context: Why Does the State Infiltrate Political Organisations?' *Verso*, 16 April 2020.

Woods, Neil. 2018. 'Exposing Undercover Policing in The U.K.' Presented at the Funzing Talk, Sink Pong.

Wynn, Natalie. 2020. 'Canceling | Contrapoints [Video]'. YouTube, 2 January 2020.

Young, Iris Marion. 2003. 'The Logic of Masculinist Protection: Reflections on the Current Security State'. *Signs* 29 (1): 1–25.

————. 2011. *Responsibility for Justice*. Oxford: Oxford University Press.

Yuval-Davis, Nira, Georgie Wemyss, and Kathryn Cassidy. 2018. 'Everyday Bordering, Belonging and the Reorientation of British Immigration Legislation'. *Sociology* 52 (2): 228–44.

KOSHKA DUFF

———

Koshka Duff is a lecturer in in social and political philosophy at the University of Nottingham.

nottingham.ac.uk/humanities/departments/philosophy/ people/koshka.duff

CAT SIMS

———

Cat Sims is a Birmingham based illustrator.

catsims.org

DOG SECTION PRESS

———

Dog Section Press is a not-for-profit publisher and distributor of seditious literature, and a registered worker-owned cooperative.

dogsection.org

Other titles from Dog Section Press:

Great Anarchists
Ruth Kinna and Clifford Harper

Animal Squat
Double Why

Make Rojava Green Again
Internationalist Commune of Rojava

The Rhyming Guide to Grenfell Britain
Potent Whisper

NO! Against Adult Supremacy
Stinney Distro

Subvertising Manual
Brandalism

Subvertising
Hogre

Advertising Shits in Your Head
Anon.

Options for dealing with squatting
Persons Unknown

Forthcoming titles from Dog Section Press:

Post-Internet Far Right
12 Rules For What?

Revenge
Clifford Harper

The Rojava Reader
Various Authors

DOPE Anthology (1-10)
Various Authors

Black Anarchism
Zoe Samudzi

DOPE MAGAZINE

DOPE Magazine is a quarterly newspaper published by Dog Section Press. Through a horizontal network of distributors around the UK, people ranging from rough sleepers to asylum seekers can collect copies for free, sell them for the cover price of £3 and keep the full proceeds.

DOPE is also free to prisoners, who can request a subscription via Haven Distribution.

Help us to get more DOPE Magazine to more people in more places by supporting our Patreon.

patreon.org/dopemag

DOG SECTION PRESS